The Alternative
HEN

Also available from Virgin Books:

The Alternative Stag

The Alternative

HEN

Kirstie Rowson & Genna Hayman

First published in Great Britain in 2003 by
Virgin Books Ltd
Thames Wharf Studios · Rainville Road · London W6 9HA
Copyright © Kirstie Rowson & Genna Hayman 2003

**Great care has been taken with this guide to be as accurate and up-to-date as
possible, but details such as addresses, telephone numbers, website and email
addresses are liable to change. The publishers and authors cannot accept
responsibility for any consequences arising from the use of this book. We
would be delighted to receive any corrections and suggestions for inclusion in
the next edition.**

ISBN 0 7535 0806 0

Designed and typeset by Lovelock & Co.
Printed and bound in Great Britain by Mackays of Chatham

Contents

For Jo and Claire, the original Alternative Hens.

Acknowledgements

We would like to thank Jo Edgerton, Claire Kennedy, Alex di Silvestro, Anand Shukla, Elliot Clark and Kim Porter for helping to make this book a reality.

The Alternative Hen

So, your friend has decided to take the plunge and get married to the man of her dreams. Or perhaps you're the one about to tie the knot! You want a send-off that a hen will never forget. A night that will be a subject of your girly gossip for years to come.

A hen night may traditionally be a blushing bride's last chance to let her hair down but it is also an opportunity to make her feel sexy and sassy and, let's not forget, the centre of attention. So if you're looking for an alternative to the traditional props of the 'L' plates and net curtain-style veil, then this book is for you!

Find out everything you need to know about arranging your Alternative Hen night. From sending out the invites and choosing where to go, to having a theme and games to play to get the party going. The planning and preparations are all part of the excitement and this book will give you plenty of inspiration.

Chicks who are organising a night or weekend for their hen will get all the ideas they need and as a hen you will find loads of tips about what to do and how to have the perfect night.

Getting the Show on the Road

Are there going to be four or fourteen of you? This is obviously your hen's call. But bear in mind you need to strike a balance between having lots of people and having the flexibility of a smaller group. Do you really want every girl your hen has ever met there or would you rather keep it to her close friends? And if you're not sure about whether to invite the mums, clear any issues up early by suggesting two hen nights, one daring one for your mates and one more civilised night out for the family and any extras. This neatly avoids any disapproving glances as your hen demonstrates her lap dancing ability.

If you're the chief chick and your hen is happy to let you take over then get her to give you a list of invitees and their contact details and take it from there. You may or may not know everyone on the list; if you don't, get in touch with them all to say hello and to work out how involved your fellow chicks want to be in the preparations.

Some girls will want to help out with everything and some will be happy just to come along for the ride. If possible try to distribute responsibilities as much as you can so everyone has a chance to get involved and share in the build-up to the big night.

A date for your diary

It's important to set a date early on to make sure everyone's got the best chance of making it. The first person to consult about this is the hen herself. Does she want to let her hair down the weekend before the wedding or a month in advance? With all the last-minute wedding plans most hens prefer to book a weekend at least a fortnight before their big day. Plan it so that everyone will be relaxed and you have enough time to organise yourselves.

Sharing the cost

Try to share the financial 'burden'. It's amazing how quickly things can add up when you are preparing and planning. It will make things easier for you if you establish the ground rules in terms of budget before you

Note to chicks

Take as much of the organisation as you can out of your hen's hands – she'll have enough to deal with organising her wedding. The more surprises she has on the night, the better.

start to organise. Perhaps offer everyone a few options of things to do so that you can sound out what they are all willing to spend. It's pointless planning a weekend revelling *Sex And The City* style in New York if nobody can afford to come!

It's perfectly acceptable to suggest a kitty for any upfront expenses or group gifts for your hen. This is also a good way of managing things on the night itself, with everybody contributing to a pool of cash that can be used to pay for the meal, rounds of drinks and entrance to the nightclub (if this is what you choose to do).

Hens on Tour – Choosing a Location

There are a few factors to consider when choosing a location for your Alternative Hen night. You may be tempted to plump for your hometown; it's easy, everyone can get there, you know where to go and it's cheap. But if at all possible try not to settle for this option, as getting away will create more of a sense of occasion and ensure it's a night to remember, rather than a night down the local. Being somewhere new or different will also make sure that you don't bump into anyone that you don't want to and, safe in this knowledge, any inhibitions you have will just fade away.

When it comes to thinking about your accommodation it's a case of the more the merrier. Remember the days of pyjama parties and midnight feasts? This is the perfect excuse to relive those memories. If a group of you need somewhere to stay, book a couple of family rooms in a hotel so you can all gossip late into the night. Most hotels cater for groups of three or four who want to share one room. In the case where there's a big group of you, book well in advance and you should be able to get rooms next to each other.

If you do decide to go out locally (and want to save your cash), arrange to stay at one of your chick's houses. Part of the fun of the morning after is sharing your hangover and dissecting every second of the night before over a greasy fry-up.

All major cities in the UK have a lot to offer in terms of nightlife and fun things to do in the day. The Alternative Activities and Events sections and the Alternative Directory at the back of this book will give you lots of pointers to help you choose where to go and what to do. You may want to visit somewhere a few of you know well, or strike out and host your festivities somewhere new. If a UK city break isn't for you, you might want to think about a weekend in the country or an overseas jaunt.

Escape to the country

If you prefer to be out of the city then find yourselves a cosy country cottage to stay in. There are hundreds of places in the UK that are let through companies or from the individuals who own them. The Internet or the Sunday supplements are the best place to start your search but you will also find some website addresses in our Alternative Activities section. You can rent out more unusual places such as a castle, mill or a tower from organisations such as the Landmark Trust (www.landmarktrust.co.uk).

Out in the countryside you are sure to have plenty of options for daytime activities in the surrounding area but check this with the local tourist board when you are choosing where to stay. Also, bear in mind that you will probably only be an hour or so away from one of the cities in the Alternative Directory, so have a look at the activity listings here as well. On the night itself you can still dress up and enjoy having a theme even if you're staying in. Turn the evening into a games extravaganza with plenty of forfeits for your hen. Then enjoy a long lazy meal with wine flowing, safe in the knowledge that you don't even have to find a cab home.

Further afield

You don't have to limit yourselves to the UK. With cheap airlines making regular flights, Europe and the USA are becoming ever more accessible. You could tempt your chicks with champagne and croissants in belle Paris, paella and jugs of sangria in sunny Barcelona, or maybe one of the ideas in the Alternative Events listings will catch your eye. Budget will probably be the main issue here but if your group feel like splashing out then going abroad will give your Alternative Hen weekend an extra special twist. Our selection of International Ideas has details of good tourist websites for major destinations that will help you to decide where to go and also to plan what to do once you get there.

Note to chicks

Things to think about when planning where to host your Alternative Hen night are:

◆ Budget – don't spend all your money on getting there and have no cash left for cocktails.

◆ Convenience – if you've got chicks travelling from all over the country to be there, consider somewhere in the middle so that it's fair to everyone.

◆ Distance and travelling time – if you've got a whole weekend then you may have more time to travel but if you've only got one night you don't want to get there just in time for last orders. On the other hand, if you do end up going somewhere further away, and you're all travelling together, be sure to make the journey part of the fun.

◆ What you want to do – if you're going clubbing, you don't want to be staying in a sleepy village miles from the action.

◆ And, perhaps most importantly, you should of course take into account where your hen wants to go!

Collecting Your Photos and Stories

Your fellow chicks will probably have known your hen through various stages of her life and so should have lots of juicy tales to tell about her. And you are all bound to have some amusing and embarrassing photos of the star of the show in various guises. Put the word out that you need all the material you can get to prepare for the big night.

There are loads of ways to use all the bits and pieces you collect. Here are some suggestions to get you started.

Forfeit cards: these are essential for your Alternative Hen night and can be personalised by sticking copies of photos on the back of the cards. Then, every time you give your hen a forfeit she will have the added pleasure of seeing a picture of herself leering drunkenly at the camera with her dodgy 80s perm and pastel bat-wing top (see 'Forfeits' chapter for more info).

Place mats: if you're going out for a meal, blow up photos to A4 size and laminate them. Use your own creations in the restaurant so that all your chicks have a *gorgeous* picture of their hen smiling up at them. If you feel like putting in some extra effort you could superimpose the heads of your hen and maybe her husband-to-be on to a selection of cheesy full-page magazine ads and laminate these instead. Use a page from a bridal magazine so your hen can have a preview of how she will look on her big day. Or how about using holiday or retirement brochures or, if you fancy, use something a bit more cheeky …

Props: use your photos wherever you can. If you're dressing up as Charlie's Angels then take it literally by making angel wings for your chicks and sticking pictures of your hen on them. If you've got nowhere else to stick a picture, make badges to wear on your tops. If you are going to be Spanish señoritas, make sure your hen's face (aged thirteen with bad hair, obviously) is staring out at you when you open your fans!

Games: you can use stories that you have collected in the ways suggested in the Games section. The juicier the better.

Speeches: while stories are essential to do your hen justice, a few choice photos will make perfect props should you decide to make a speech (see 'Making an Alternative Speech' for more ideas).

Keepsakes: it's great for your hen to have some pressies to take away with her and if you're feeling creative make her a keepsake book or photo album. You might want to include reminders of her single days and notorious quotes and memories from her past. Alternatively, go the whole hog and give the hen her very own *This Is Your Life* experience complete with show host and Big Red Book. The more effort you make with this treasured memento, the better, as it will sum up everything your hen has meant to you until now.

Forfeits

No Alternative Hen night would be complete without forfeits. They are the rite of passage for your hen and give her a licence to flirt to ensure that she is the centre of attention. Men will flock like moths to a flame when they see a group of girls in fancy dress doing forfeits.

Eight to ten is the ideal number of forfeits for your night out. Write each one on a separate small piece of card and put each of them in an envelope so that you have the added dramatic effect of your hen having to rip them open.

Elaborately fan out the forfeits for your hen to choose one and male eyes a-plenty will flicker in your direction. If a character is identified in a challenge, use your imagination about who they might be; that is, find a likely looking man in the vicinity to help your hen fulfil the task. You will have no shortage of willing participants! You can use your forfeits randomly throughout the night or issue one each time you get another round in. Inevitably the rationing of forfeits will spiral out of control as the night goes on and you will find yourselves doing one after another. But if you want to be extra sneaky keep a couple of the more raunchy ones back as your hen is bound to get more daring as the night draws on … although preferably not to the point where she has to call off her wedding …

Note to chicks

Depending on how lenient you are feeling, let your hen have a joker card that she can use if she wants to pass on a forfeit – but only one. So, once she's passed on one forfeit, she's got to do all the others.

In the next chapter, we discuss themes and have given each its own specific forfeits, which can be easily adapted if you are feeling creative. Or you can of course create some of your own that are specific to your hen by getting each of the chicks to use her imagination and write a tailor-made one on the night.

Themes

One of the keys to a successful Alternative Hen night is having a theme. You'll find that this will make the whole experience take on a life of its own. We've given you ten to spark your imagination, with ideas for outfits, forfeits for your hen and even suggestions for props and drinks in order to stay in character. All of them see the hen in her own unique ensemble while the chicks all wear the same outfit for maximum impact. You can tailor any of these to create a totally personalised night and can even use the theme to influence the whole experience, from the activities and restaurant you choose to the club you go to.

Giving the night a theme will allow your hen and chicks to be in disguise and in character. You will be amazed at how your friends suddenly show a whole different side to their personalities once they are dressed up. This is a licence to be as enthusiastic as you like, to go completely over the top and, most importantly of course, to flirt like crazy.

You know better than anyone what theme will be most suited to your hen. Let your imagination run wild on this one. Think about what your hen enjoys, which celebs she's fancied or dreamt about, her favourite film or TV show and stories from her past. This is her chance to get completely into character (and maybe even live out a fantasy), so pay attention to every detail. Think about your make-up and hairstyles. Sprinkle some glitter, use fake tattoos and accessorise as much as possible to complete your outfits. Mascara is all well and good but put on a pair of false eyelashes and you will be batting your eyelids for Britain. All the better for getting the attention you deserve.

Keep your theme a secret from your hen if possible. Then on the night you can blindfold her and lay out her outfit so that it can be revealed in all its glory. Don't forget to take a photo of her reaction. And then, just like you used to, you can all have the fun of getting ready together for your ultimate girly night out.

Note to chicks

Never underestimate the power of the wig! Put any girl in a wig and you will see a transformation right in front of your eyes. You can buy a whole variety of gorgeous locks from most party shops. It doesn't matter if the wig doesn't look quite as you'd imagined on your hen – it will quickly become a vital part of the night's festivities. Pammy Anderson may bear more resemblance to a Lily Savage/Dolly Parton hybrid, and Farrah Fawcett might look like Jimmy Saville, but either way you'll never look at your hen in quite the same way again.

Baywatch/
Henwatch Babes

Picture yourselves on a shimmering Californian beach running in slow motion as the muscular beach hunks gasp in admiration ... Then get back to reality and picture yourselves running in slow motion down the high street, looking oh-so-sexy with your American tan and ready to rescue any man from drowning in his beer.

Outfit
- Long, blonde, curly wig to make your hen look like an extra special *Baywatch* babe.
- Everyone should wear red vest tops (or swimsuits depending on how daring you're feeling) and blue shorts or cut-off trousers.
- Flip-flops.
- Instant fake tan (or American tan tights – but you may find it a bit tricky to get your flip-flops on so wear trainers instead).

Drink
Sex-on-the-Beach cocktails.

Props

◆ Floats – these will really complete your look. Make your floats by getting creative with some papier-mâché and empty squash bottles, painting them red and attaching a black strap to sling them over your shoulders.

◆ Scissors (for one of the forfeits).

Forfeits

◆ You're showing the extras how it's done. Demonstrate a slow motion 'Henwatch' run across the bar.

◆ A victim is drowning in his drink! Get him to buy you a drink so you can show him some safe drinking techniques.

Extra effort

◆ David Hasslehoff mask – make these for each of your chicks by backing a colour photocopy of David's face with cardboard and sticking a straw on the reverse so that you can hold the mask to your face (you can use these to turn every man you meet in to a beach hunk). Hassle on!

◆ 'Henwatch' badge – draw your own 'Henwatch' logo and use a fetching photo of your hen in a bikini to complete the badge.

- You're overheating on the beach – find a bronzed hunk of a man to cool you off with an ice cube.

- Tonight is a rockin' beach party. Practise your limbo under two men's joined arms.

- You're a beautiful babe. The camera loves you. Pout and pose for someone else's photo.

- You know they're real, we know they're real. Have a stranger confirm it!

- Your contract at 'Henwatch' is up for renewal. Prove your worth by claiming as many labels from men's underwear as you can in the next five minutes. (You'll need the scissors for this one.)

- The Californian heat is getting to you. Cool yourself off seductively with an ice cube.

- You spot a loner on the beach. Introduce him to the show by asking if he needs to be rescued.

- You're taking photos for the 'Henwatch' catalogue and you need male models. Go and find some and get snapping!

Beauty Queen and Attendants

For you glamour pusses out there, if your hen is always the belle of the ball then treat her to a night as a beauty queen – tiara and all. As her attendants you will have the perfect excuse to fuss around her all night; consider it good practice for her wedding day …

Outfit

◆ A foxy, glamorous dress and sparkly tiara for your beauty queen hen.

◆ Sash with 'Miss Hen Party 200X' for the hen (change year or name as appropriate) and 'Hen Attendant' for the chicks – make these out of pieces of silky material with words either sewn on or stencilled in marker pen.

◆ Chicks or 'attendants', as you should be known throughout the night, should all wear similar glamorous outfits.

◆ Immaculate make-up.

Props

◆ Make-up for reapplying to perfection throughout the night.

◆ Acceptance speech for your beauty queen (for one of the forfeits).

Drink

Champagne.

Forfeits

◆ One of the judges at the bar has a particular passion for tap dancing. Try to get a drink out of him by wowing him with your efforts.

◆ You're a role model and a giver in life – be a taker. Convince a stranger in the bar to buy you a drink and let him administer it to you however he sees fit.

◆ The heat and glare of the lights is getting to you – cool yourself off at the bar with an ice cube.

Extra effort

Score cards – write the numbers 1–10 on pieces of white card so that you can mark your hen on her forfeit performances. Ideally, make a set for each chick so you can all have a go at scoring ...

◆ You're looking for a sugar daddy. Approach a candidate of your attendants' choice and chat him up with the line, 'Diamonds are a girl's best friend; have you got any jewels worth admiring?'

◆ You haven't told anyone in the contest that you used to be a pole dancer. Find a pole and let your shady past catch up with you as you show your attendants your special skills.

◆ Approach a group of admirers and deliver your winning acceptance speech. (*Note to chicks*: you will need to write this for your hen in advance.)

◆ It's time for the swimwear section, but you've lost your bikini bottoms. Get a suitable replacement from a charming young man. Boxers, briefs, Y-fronts or a thong will do!

◆ Get your vanity case out and practise your make-up routine on a willing male volunteer.

◆ Congratulations! You've won a modelling contract. Practise your catwalk strut with a male model of your choice. Make sure the photographers get some good shots.

◆ Get a free drink using only your pout and poise.

Wild West – Sheriff and Cowgirls

Ye-har! Whoa there, Tonto! Sling on your chaps and holster and gallop into town. The perfect excuse to lasso all those studs and down whiskies at the bar. Let your hen don her sheriff's badge for the night and run all those low-life outlaws out of town.

Outfit

◆ Sheriff's badge and a Dolly Parton wig for your hen.

◆ Lots of denim, suede and tassels – short skirts or sexy low-slung jeans.

◆ Cowgirl hat – make your hen stand out with a bit of added sparkle on her hat for that rodeo star effect.

◆ Remember chicks, you all need to look as similar as possible so that your hen is singled out.

Props

◆ Water pistols in holsters.

◆ Scissors (for one of the forfeits).

◆ Lasso – to catch all those gorgeous stallions.
◆ Catchphrase – practise your Texan accent and say 'Hey there, cowboy' to every man you meet.

Drink

Beer to start the night, moving on to hard liquor.

Forfeits

◆ There's an outlaw in town. Challenge him to a shot duel. Line up a couple of shots and see who can down them fastest.
◆ You've lost your spurs! Prove your worth by retrieving as many labels from men's pants as you can in two minutes. (You'll need the scissors for this one.)
◆ Show your deputy cowgirls your 'riding' technique. Get a man down on all fours if you're brave enough, or use a chair to lap dance.

- You spot a seductive stranger in the bar. Approach him and say, 'You're not from round these parts are you? Well, I'm the sheriff and I need to know, is that a gun in your pocket or are you just pleased to see me?'

- You need to practise your bucking bronco for the county show. Get a piggyback from a cowboy and stay on as long as you can.

- Rope in as many steeds as possible and brand them with your lipstick kiss – you've got a minute starting *now*!

- Find an outlaw in the bar and bring him back tethered to claim your reward. He can get himself out of jail by buying you a drink.

- Some of the cowboys can't handle their liquor. To prevent a bar brawl douse down those hot-blooded males with a water pistol.

- One of your deputies is getting a bit too big for her boots. Challenge her to an arm wrestle to prove your status as sheriff.

- Swagger up to Willy the Wasted, the town troublemaker. Let him know this town ain't big enough for the both of you … he can only stay if he buys you a beer.

Charlie's Angels and Devils

Charlie's got a mission for you, so dig out your flares and platforms, you disco divas. What better excuse do you need to flick your hair like Farrah Fawcett and smother yourselves with glitter?

Outfit

◆ Farrah Fawcett-style wig for your hen – you can buy a party wig with straight hair and use curlers and *lots* of hairspray to get the 70s effect. Just don't make the mistake of melting the hair.

◆ Angel wings – you can buy these from a party shop or make your own with cut-out cardboard and elastic. Don't forget to finish them off with a suitably mortifying picture of your hen stuck on for extra effect.

◆ Flares for hen – preferably white for the blushing bride.

◆ Black flares for the chicks.

◆ Foxy, 70s-style tops – the hen should be in white and all the chicks in red.

Props

◆ Water pistols – the ultimate *Charlie's Angels* accessory.

◆ Devil's horns for chicks.

◆ Farrah flicks all round – bring along a hot brush to create those 70s flicks before you hit the town.

Drink

Babycham.

Forfeits

◆ Your culprit is renowned for wearing red Y-fronts. Demand that your suspect shows you his underpants so you can eliminate him from your inquiries.

◆ Give a man a full body frisk and see if he's packing a weapon.

◆ Charlie has given you a catchphrase to recognise your allies. Smile at every man you meet and say, 'Man, you're too hot to handle!' If they smile back they are one of Charlie's.

◆ Get the barman's attention using only your sexy 70s moves so that you can order your next round. Get your fellow angels to back you up.

◆ Find a foxy man to buy you a drink. You don't want to leave any fingerprints so get him to feed you the drink however he chooses.

- ◆ Take your suspects by surprise and run into the next bar brandishing your water pistol, ready for action!
- ◆ For your next mission you will be disguised as a mechanic. Practise your lines and get into character by asking a man if you can 'tighten his nuts'.
- ◆ Practise your chat-up technique with the same line you used to win Charlie over: 'Is that a gun in your pocket or are you just pleased to see me?'
- ◆ Your suspect is a high-kicking champion. Challenge strangers to a high-kicking competition to eliminate suspects. (Try not to end up in casualty.)
- ◆ Find two gorgeous men to strike a *Charlie's Angels* pose with you. Get photographic evidence.

Bond Girls

007 may be the smoothest secret agent but it's the Bond girls who keep his adrenaline rushing. Never shaken but certainly causing a stir.

Outfit

◆ Hen should be dressed as one of the more memorable Bond girls such as Honey Ryder, Pussy Galore, Octopussy or Solitaire, while all the chicks are dressed the same as one of the others. Check out Bond sites on the web for a bit of inspiration.

◆ Or dress your chicks as Miss Moneypenny so your hen can really stand out as the only Bond girl.

Props

◆ Water pistols.
◆ Gadgets.

Drink

Martinis (shaken not stirred of course).

Forfeits

◆ There's a double agent in the bar. You know he's wearing Calvin Klein underwear so check as many labels as you have to, to find the right man.

◆ Use your Bond girl charms to get a drink from the barman without saying a word.

◆ Synchronise watches … you have two minutes to get kisses from ten men in the bar.

◆ Convince a Bond in the bar to re-enact the opening scene while you become his silhouetted dancer. Get your chicks to sing your theme tune.

◆ Crush a man between your 'Onatopp' thighs until he agrees to buy you a drink.

◆ Charm a dashing stranger by whispering, '*I've* got the gun in *my* pocket so you must just be pleased to see me …'

◆ Use this classic Bond theme to tell the barman how much he is appreciated, by singing him the opening verse of 'Nobody Does It Better'.

◆ Name ten Bond films or drink a tequila shot.

Cops aka Hen Patrol

Take control of the town and make your own laws as the Hen Patrol. Just don't get yourselves arrested for impersonating police officers.

Outfit

◆ Full fancy dress police uniform if possible, but with a sassy edge.

◆ Differentiate your hen by getting her to wear a basque under her jacket instead of a blouse.

◆ Improvise where you need to – you can wear short black skirts and white blouses and you will be able to buy any props you need from party shops or fancy dress shops.

◆ Policewomen's hats.

Props

◆ Furry handcuffs for the hen to help her arrest men for various crimes.

◆ Badges with your hen's face on to prove you are part of the Hen Patrol.

◆ Phallic object (for one of the forfeits).

Drink

Anything you like, you're off duty!

Forfeits

◆ Your suspect has a tattoo – track him down and make sure he proves it to you.

◆ Handcuff a man and lead him to your chicks for interrogation. He can only be released when he buys you a drink of your choice.

◆ You're on an international mission disguised as a salsa dancer. Grab a man and impress him with your salsa steps to keep up your disguise.

◆ You're thinking of moonlighting as a policewoman stripper. Practise your pole dancing technique in the bar.

◆ Your chicks look to you for advice – demonstrate the perfect way to handle a weapon. (You'll need your phallic object for this one.)

◆ You're in charge of an identity parade but decide to steady your suspects' nerves with a drink. Line up your men, head to head with your chicks, and challenge them to a drinking race, domino style. (Each chick and 'suspect' must down their drink before the next one in the line can start drinking.)

◆ Use this classic line to impress a male plain-clothes officer in the bar: 'Is that a truncheon in your pocket, officer, or are you just pleased to see me?'

Spanish Salsa Queen and her Señoritas

Click those castanets and shake your maracas! If your hen fancies herself as a sultry Spanish señorita then get your frills on and salsa the night away in the steamy Mediterranean heat (well, in the sweaty nightclub anyway).

Outfit

◆ Lots of frills and plunging necklines. Differentiate your hen by dressing her in red while all the chicks wear either black or white.

◆ Heeled shoes to tap impressively as you salsa.

◆ Lots of gold jewellery – big gold earrings and jangly gold bracelets.

Props

◆ Fans for that sultry flamenco feel – with a photo of your hen plastered on one side.

◆ A single red rose (for one of the forfeits).

Drink

Sangria for starters and tequila shots for afters.

Forfeits

◆ The bar is hot and humid. Use this to your advantage and approach a sultry stranger, saying 'Man, you're hot!' as you waft him with your fan.

◆ You want to spread your Spanish influence. Find a willing partner and teach him to salsa.

◆ Make use of your musical talents and convince a sexy señor to buy you a drink by shaking your maracas.

◆ Using only your alluring Spanish eyes, get a man to take a rose from your teeth.

◆ The Mediterranean sun is getting to you. Cool yourself down seductively with an ice cube.

◆ You've enflamed the Spanish passions of two men in the bar but you can't choose between them – so get them to arm wrestle for your affections.

◆ You know you are the flamenco queen, so prove it to your fellow señoritas by having a dance-off with them one by one.

◆ You've got gypsy blood from a distant generation. Tell the barman you will read his palm and tell him his fortune for a free drink.

◆ Impress the locals and let them know who you really are: '*Soy un campeón de flamenco, ven a bailar conmígo!*' (I'm a flamenco champion, come dance with me!)

Sandy and her Pink Ladies

Tell me about it, stud … *If you're looking for an all-singing all-dancing Alternative Hen night, this is the theme for you. Show me a girl who doesn't know all the words to 'Summer Lovin'' …*

Outfit

◆ Dress your hen in a slinky black catsuit or as 50s-style virgin Sandy – whichever you think is more suitable for her personality.

◆ Chicks should all be in black Capri pants or 50s skirts with pink tops.

◆ White ankle socks.

Props

◆ Pink lipstick for the perfect pout.

◆ Chew gum with attitude.

◆ High ponytails with pink bows.

◆ Hen's face on button badges.

◆ Comb (for one of the forfeits).

Drink

Daiquiris – drink them like milkshakes.

Forfeits

◆ Re-enact Sandy's breakthrough moment by finding your own Danny Zucko. Throw a cigarette on the floor and stub it out with your toe, saying, 'Tell me about it, stud.'

◆ You feel like having a moment to yourself. Wander down the street to the next bar singing 'Hopelessly Devoted to You' as you stare wistfully at the stars.

◆ Guys these days just have no style. Take a comb and show a wannabe T-Bird how to achieve a Kenicky quiff.

◆ The school magazine is running a model competition and you're keen to fit in. Have your photo taken as you lounge seductively across a car bonnet.

◆ You're getting sick of your virginal Sandy image and are desperate to be a Pink Lady – prove your sexual prowess by heading off into the bar and coming back with an item of men's underwear.

◆ Find the jukebox (aka the DJ) and request 'Summer Lovin'' or 'You're The One That I Want'. Find a Danny to dance and sing with you.

- They had the cheek to sing it behind your back so get your Pink Ladies to give you a rousing chorus of 'Look at me I'm Sandra Dee'.

- You need to practise for the high school dance-off. Find a cute T-Bird and ask him if you can interest him in a hand-jive.

- School's out! Shake your pom-poms and give the bar a hen night cheer – 'Give me an H!'

- It's getting steamy at the drive-in. Take a leaf out of Rizzo's flirtation book and cool yourself off flirtatiously with an ice cube.

Fame/Flashdance

Fame costs, and right here's where you start paying… in sweat! *If you long for the heyday of legwarmers and Leroy then practise your high kicks and become an 80s dance troupe for the night. Pans People had better watch their backs as you split leap into town.*

Outfits

◆ Leggings, leotards and legwarmers.

◆ Hen wears one bright colour from head to toe while chicks all wear a darker colour so your hen stands out as the dance troupe leader.

◆ Wig for your hen – 80s body perm style.

◆ High ponytails.

◆ Sweatbands.

Props

◆ 80s make-up.

◆ Glitter galore.

Drink

Vodka and Redbull to keep your energy levels up for all that dancing.

Make up a dance routine in the daytime to wow the crowds later in the club.

Forfeits

◆ Stop the traffic and grapevine across a zebra crossing.

◆ Have a go at some body popping and send the electricity down the line of chicks. Try to keep it flowing through the bar.

◆ It's head to head, boys versus girls, on the dance floor. See who can do the most complete 360-degree jump.

◆ You're the head dancer. Teach your chicks one of your best dance moves for a cocktail of your choice.

◆ Your moonwalk could give Michael Jackson a run for his money. Challenge a man to moonwalk to the bar. The first one there buys the other a drink.

◆ Lead your chicks as you gracefully split leap down the road to the next bar.

◆ Hey, sexy lady! Shimmy your shoulders at the barman until he gives you a free drink.

◆ Take a well-earned rest and loan a man your legwarmers. Get him to entertain you while you cheer him on.

Roman Goddess and Attendants

Friends, Romans, countrymen … If sipping red wine out of goblets and being fed grapes by gorgeous tanned men is your hen's thing then transform her into a Roman goddess for the night. You can all fuss around her as her attendants – just try not to let your precariously secured togas reveal more than you want them to.

Outfits

◆ White sheet togas.

◆ Laurel crown and golden rope belt for your goddess of a hen.

◆ Sandals.

Props

◆ Grapes.

◆ Eye pencil (for one of the forfeits).

Drink

Red wine from goblets.

Forfeits

◆ Have a chariot race to the next bar against your chief bridesmaid. Unfortunately you've forgotten your chariots so you will have to make do with piggybacks from 'gods' that you find in the bar.

◆ Your attendants are helping you to stay pure and strong in body and mind. Prove your status by challenging one of them to an arm wrestle.

◆ You're looking for a new male attendant. Get three men to strip to the waist and pick the best one to buy you a drink. (If they're feeling a bit shy you can tell a lot from their biceps.)

◆ Ask an Adonis to feed you grapes as you strike a reclining pose.

◆ You need to rest your weary sandalled feet. Get a willing gladiator to get down on all fours and be your footrest while you sip from a goblet of wine.

◆ You need to recruit new gladiators but some of them are looking rather faint-hearted. Improve their masculinity by drawing chest hair on a candidate with your eye pencil.

◆ As a goddess you cannot possibly walk to the bar. Ask two strong gladiators to carry you in your seat so that they can order you a drink.

◆ Audition men to be your Caesar. Strong men have hard nipples, so check a few candidates until you find your man.

More Inspiration for Themes

If you don't fancy being quite so elaborate or if you don't have much time to organise yourselves, you can always keep your theme as simple as wearing the colour pink or asking everyone to wear feather boas. But as this is a once in a lifetime opportunity to go completely over the top, try to persuade your hen to take advantage and dress up to the nines. Here are some additional themes that might spark your imaginations.

Buffy the Vampire Slayer

A good one for a high-kicking hen night around Hallowe'en but this theme will provide plenty of entertainment at any time of the year. Your hen can ooze Buffy's sex appeal, complete with crucifix, while the rest of you dress as gothic vamps, with fangs of course. Don't forget lashings of holy water or, failing that, vodka.

Cheerleaders

A variation on the classic schoolgirl theme. Short skirts and knee-high socks, bunches and pom-poms. Use transfers to emblazon a picture of your hen across your chests and cheer her on as she leads you with a cheerleader chant through town.

Ghosts of Fashions Past

Choose the 60s, 70s or 80s as your theme and dress accordingly. Be as stylish or as over the top as you like and find a nightclub or karaoke bar that will enhance your theme with music from that era.

Film Stars

Choose your hen's favourite female film icon and mould your theme around her. How about Marilyn Monroe, Lara Croft, Wonder Woman, Audrey Hepburn or Princess Leia? There are endless possibilities!

Moulin Rouge

A lavish and dramatic theme where you can go as over the top as you like. Stick on your false eyelashes, pull on your silk gloves and breathe in to squeeze into your bustier. Dress your hen with extra glitz to give her 'sparkling diamond' status.

Music Icons

Focus on your hen's favourite pop star and build this in to your theme. Madonna is a great example as she has many different looks to choose from. Dress your hen as one of Madonna's incarnations while all the chicks dress as one of the others. Choose from her 'Like A Virgin' phase, conical breasts phase or suited–booted 'Vogue' phase. Enhance this theme by making a karaoke bar part of your night so your hen can live out her fantasies and sing the hits of her icon to her heart's content.

Space Age

Simple but effective: wear as much silver as you can lay your hands on and slap glitter on every bit of exposed flesh. Spend the night running around with your laser gun tracking down alien life forms.

Making an Alternative Speech

Wedding speeches are traditionally best man territory but it's getting more common for the chief bridesmaid to want to have her say. And speeches don't have to be reserved for the wedding day. The hen night is a great opportunity to make a tailored speech just for the girls and say everything that you can't say in front of the bride's grandparents. You may not get a chance to do it at the wedding (or you may not want to!) and it's the perfect time to showcase some of the best stories and photos that you have. If the idea fills you with dread, remember, there is no doubt that she will love it. And it doesn't have to just be the chief bridesmaid – this is a chance for any chick who wants to, to stand up and say a few words.

Of course, a speech about your hen is going to be a very personal thing but if you want to make one and are stuck for ideas, here are a few pointers to get you started:

Ex-boyfriends: there is always some good material with this subject, especially when supported by photos (enlarged for easy viewing obviously) … just exactly *why* did she ever go out with the floppy-fringed, spotty boy when she was sixteen?

School days: you can use lots of anecdotes here from your classroom days. Mention her old nicknames or her massive crush on Morten Harket/Gary Barlow or the head boy; also remind her of that poodle perm she had when she was fifteen and shocking fashion mistakes such as puff-ball skirts and bat-wing jumpers.

Her fiancé: think of any silly stories about her loved one, mention cutesy names he calls her or surprise everyone with a few choice photos of him looking suitably gorgeous. Try to get hold of some pictures of him as a kid or teenager from his mum or mates with the worst hair-do you've ever seen.

Mr and Mrs: if you want to turn your speech into more of a two-way game with your hen, this is an ideal time to act as quizmaster (for details see the Games Galore section).

The slushy bit: it's really nice to start or end your speech on a slightly more serious note with a mention of what you all love about your friend – let her know how happy you are for her and raise a glass for a toast to your Alternative Hen.

Games Galore

As well as having a theme and forfeits for the hen, you can speckle your weekend with games. Use one or two of these games to get your chicks bonding if they don't know each other and to liven up any quieter gals. Here are some suggestions that will get you all talking and will make sure you discover a few cheeky facts about each other. Some involve alcohol and some don't, but you can turn pretty much any of these into a drinking game with a bit of imagination.

Just to clarify, for those of you that haven't left the house in the past twenty years, in terms of drinking fines a 'finger' is the width of your finger from the top of the level of your drink in your glass. Big hands? Bad luck.

Alphabet Game

Best played: with a group of close-knit friends on the journey there

This game is very straightforward: you simply work your way through the alphabet naming past conquests of either the bride-to-be or your fellow chicks. As you try to think of someone for every letter you will be amazed by how many dodgy guys from the past will come back to you. Gorgeously cringe-making! The main object is obviously to embarrass the hell out of your hen but at least she will have a chance to get you back for once.

Animal Noises

Best played: in the bar

This game will cause much hilarity as you neigh and growl your way round the circle. The first person starts with the phrase, 'I went to the zoo and I saw a …' They must then make the sound of an animal that they might see there. The next person then repeats the phrase and makes the first person's noise and then adds another. The game goes on round your circle, adding more and more animal noises until someone messes up and has to drink a two-finger fine. Then you start all over again.

Bunny Rabbits

Best played: in the bar

Sit round a table and start with your hen as head bunny girl. She puts her hands to her head like bunny ears and twitches her nose. The chick on each side of her must twitch their noses as her fellow bunnies and dig imaginary burrows with their hands. The hen then 'throws' the role of head bunny across to another chick by pointing her bunny ears (i.e. hands) in that direction. The new head bunny puts her hands/bunny ears to her head and twitches her nose while those on either side of her twitch their noses in support and dig their burrows. Whenever anyone messes up they must drink. The 'throws' get faster and faster and twitching noses will get more frantic until you dissolve into a giggling heap of chicks! You can also add extra drinking rules to make it even more difficult to keep up (see 'Additional Drinking Rules').

Dark Horses

Best played: over a meal, perhaps at lunchtime before the night

This is another great game to help bond your group of chicks and it also tests your hen's knowledge of her friends. Again this requires a little preparation and someone to play quizmaster to pose the questions to the hen. Ask each of your chicks to write down a couple of cheeky facts about themselves without telling anyone else. These can be things they have done or fun secrets about themselves that your hen will not necessarily know. Gather up all the bits of paper and then read them out to the hen one by one. Tell her that each is a fact about someone in the group and she then has to guess who you are talking about. The more risqué or amusing the facts, the better.

For example: one of your chicks was once rather drunk and really needed to go to the loo when she was walking home, so she went quickly behind a hedge. It was only when she got up to walk away she realised that she had gone by the only gap in the hedge and had shown her bare buttocks to all the passing traffic ... which of your chicks was it that pulled a full moon?

Fuzzy Duck

Best played: in the bar

It doesn't take a genius to work out what you'll end up saying here, but it's still a good warm-up when you first get out. You need to be in a circle to start. The idea is that the first player says 'Fuzzy Duck' and the person on her left then chooses whether to carry on saying 'Fuzzy Duck', in which case play continues, or 'Does he?' in which case play changes direction. Once the direction changes to be anticlockwise, the next player has the choice of saying 'Ducky Fuzz', for play to continue, or 'Does he?' to change direction again. It's good to get it flying around the table and not looking at the person who's meant to go next to make it more likely that they will mess up their turn. Anyone that misses their cue or says the wrong thing must drink a two-finger fine, so obviously speed is of the essence.

Hen Wave

Best played: in the bar

A simple but very effective game for getting you all plastered, this is a drinking version of the traditional Mexican wave. Keep an eye on what your other chicks are drinking and when you think you have the least left call a Hen Wave. One rule though, you must all have at least half your drink left. Each member of the group has to down their drinks one by one with the caller downing theirs first. Throughout the night each chick can only call a wave once. All the more effective if each chick stands on their chair when they down their drink but try not to get chucked out of the bar!

I Have Never …

Best played: over dinner or drinks to bond the group

This well-known game is best played when you all have a drink in your hand and are waiting for your meal to arrive, as it is perfect for getting to know everyone's sordid past. The hen starts this game with the statement, 'I have never …' She states something that she has never done, for example, 'I have never kissed two different men in the same night.' Those chicks around the table who have done this must now take a sip of their drinks. The next chick around the table then has her turn. As your friends take subtle sips of their drinks in admittance to what they have done (after the gasps of disbelief have died down), you can call upon each of them to tell the whole story about their escapades. This game is even more amusing if you are able to set people up, in particular, of course, your hen. When it is your turn say, 'I have never…' and mention something that you haven't done but you know the hen has …

Mr and Mrs

Best played: during the speech if one of your chicks chooses to make one

This game needs a little preparation but it's worth it. Also, it will only work if you know you can trust your hen's fiancé to keep his part in it a secret. Call him up when you know your hen is out and get answers to ten or twenty personal questions about the two of them as a couple. There are a few suggestions below. Write your questions on a piece of card with a fitting photo of your hen on the back for your chicks to chuckle at. One of your chicks is then the quizmaster and will ask your hen the questions but, instead of her response, she needs to answer with what she thinks her husband-to-be will have answered. Tot up how many she has answered correctly and decide on a forfeit for the number she gets wrong.

Note to chicks: you can be quite cunning with this game and make sure that she has to do the forfeit whatever the outcome ... well, nobody said you had to be an angel.

Suggested questions:

◆ What does he say is your most embarrassing memory?

◆ How often does he say he does the cleaning?

◆ Who is his ultimate super-hero?

◆ What does he think is the sweetest thing you've ever done for him?

◆ How many times a week does he say you have sex?

◆ What was the first thing he ever said to you?

◆ What does he think your favourite sexual position is?

- What does he think is your ideal Sunday morning activity?
- Who did he say you would most fancy, David Beckham or George Clooney?

Nags

Best played: in the bar

This game is based on the idea of horse racing, where the 'nags' are peanuts and the course is a pint of beer. You will therefore need a packet of salted peanuts to be your nags and a 'race' pint. All the players sit around the table with the race pint in the middle. Each player has a 'nag' (i.e. a peanut) to race. One player makes a bet – the first to reach the bottom of the race pint wins, for example. (You can make different bets each time so everyone gets a go at a wager.)

On the starter's orders all players drop their 'nags' into the race pint and keep an eye on theirs to see if they win or lose. In this case the last one to reach the bottom of the pint or to not reach it at all has to down a finger of their drink. All sorts of tactics can be involved, for example, peanuts drop at different rates depending on how much salt they have on them so players can lick it off to streamline their filly. Tasteful. Players can 'buy' another nag from the stable (the packet of peanuts) by drinking another two fingers. If a player's nag breaks in half while racing, that player must down their drink.

Pin the Willy on the Body

Best played: in the hotel room with a glass of wine before you go out

An Alternative Hen version of the good old party game, Pin the Tail on the Donkey. Buy a teenage magazine or similar to get a big poster of a guy (or you can draw your own if you're feeling artistic…). Obviously the poster must be a full-length picture or at least feature the vital area of the guy's body. The hen must then show off her artistic skills and draw a shapely willy on a piece of card and cut it out. She is then blindfolded and spun round in true 'party-game' style and must stick it on to the poster as correctly as she can. Everyone can have a go at this, and you can all draw your very own cardboard willies to stick on. Perhaps you could even give the willies the names of your hen's past conquests. Classy.

Play Your Numbers Right

Best played: in the bar

This is best played with a larger group and is a simple game that will get everyone drinking. Your hen goes first and starts by saying 'one'. Then, someone else in the group says 'two'. There is no order for who has to follow who. The point is that people have to randomly say the next consecutive number. The twist being that if two people speak at the same time, they must both drink two fingers and the numbers start again at one. If no one says anything after about a second, the person who said the last number shouts 'Nil!' Then she can give a two-finger fine to whichever player she chooses (probably the really quiet one who thinks she's being sneaky trying to sit this one out). If anyone says a number at the same time that 'nil' is said, they automatically get a two-finger fine anyway. Then the game starts again at one. An allotted chairwoman can rule over reasonable hesitation times.

Skeletons in the Closet

Best played: the night before or in the daytime

If your hen has had a rather active past (?!) and has lots of stories to tell about past boyfriends and snogs then this game is a lot of fun. Make a list of the men she has had in her life (even from schooldays holding hands in the playground) and think of a prop for each one. Put all the props in a bag and let her pick them out one by one like a lucky dip. She has to guess who the man in question is from the prop she has in her hand.

Note to chicks: if the subject of ex-boyfriends is something your hen would rather not discuss then perhaps give this one a miss. You don't want her storming off in a huff halfway through her hen weekend.

Tabloid Headlines

Best played: the night before or in the daytime

Take ten of the juiciest stories that you have about your friend and imagine they are being reported in a tabloid newspaper. What would the headlines be? Write down a headline for each, making them as cryptic as you can. For example, a story about your hen singing karaoke totally out of tune could have the headline 'Queen Of The Mike?' or a story about her antics with the head boy at school could be titled 'Student Heading For Sex-cess' – as these examples suggest, the cheesier the better.

Put the headlines in a bowl or hat and ask your hen to pick one out at a time. She has one minute to guess what sordid or funny story from her past you are reporting. If she guesses the story, she gets to tell it herself in her own words. If she doesn't guess it, she must drink a shot and one of the chicks gets to tell the story in *her* own words and must not spare any detail.

Thrupennies

Best played: in the bar

Another easy one, similar to the age-old matchbox game. You'll need two coins and a flat surface. Sit in a circle and take it in turns to throw both coins up in the air. Everyone has a turn, and the order is clockwise around the circle. How the pennies land each time, will determine the penalty:

◆ A head and a tail – the thrower is off the hook. The coins pass on to the next player without any penalty.

◆ Two heads – the player drinks a two-finger fine.

- ◆ Two tails – the player makes an additional rule or can choose to pass an immediate two-finger fine on to one of her fellow players. Play still continues with the next player in the circle.
- ◆ Anywhere other than the flat surface, the player has to down whatever is left of their drink at that time before play continues.

The Matchbox Game

Best played: in the bar

A simple game with fast results. Sit in a circle around a flat surface and take it in turns to throw a matchbox up in the air. Everyone must have a turn, going clockwise around the circle. How the matchbox lands each time it is thrown determines the drinking fine that needs to be taken or passed on to the next thrower. In short, if the matchbox lands on the:

- ◆ long edge, it accumulates a one-finger fine and passes to the next player;
- ◆ short edge, it accumulates a two-finger fine and passes to the next player, or the thrower gets to make up a new drinking rule (see 'Additional Drinking Rules' for ideas);
- ◆ large face, the player has to drink the accumulated fine and is checked by Ms Weights and Measures (see 'Additional Drinking Rules') where necessary. The game only restarts when she has done this, so it's an incentive to do it quickly. If there is no fine then the matchbox carries on to the next player in the circle;

◆ floor, bag, leg, breast or anywhere other than the flat surface, the player has to down whatever is left of their drink at that time.

Thumper

Best played: in the bar

Each of your chicks must think of a gesture to represent themselves in the game (for example, rolling their eyes or blowing a kiss). After everyone has decided on a gesture, go through them so that you can see what you're all doing. Everyone then begins drumming on the table and the hen starts proceedings by asking, 'What is the name of the game?' to which everyone replies, 'Thumper!' The hen then asks, 'Why do we play it?' and everyone replies, 'To get messed up!' Then the hen does her gesture and then someone else's. That someone else must then do their gesture and then another person's. Keep drumming on the table. The first person to mess up drinks a fine, which is decided on by the chief bridesmaid.

Who's at the Altar?

Best played: the night before

You will need a few of you for this game as you will need to split into teams. Everyone writes down ten names of people, who are either famous or well known to you all, on separate pieces of paper. Each of these names should be somehow related to weddings or marriage, perhaps celebrities who have recently married or are famous as part of a couple. Put all the names into a bag or hat.

The first team nominates one member to go first. This person has one minute to take names out of the hat and describe them to her teammates in as many words as she likes as long as she doesn't say any part of the name or any variation on it. For example, if the name on the paper is 'Brad Pitt' then she might say, 'Gorgeous film star cowboy from *Thelma and Louise*, married to one of the *Friends*.' If her team do not guess correctly she must put the name back in the hat without revealing the answer. She can also choose to put the name back in the hat if there are just no words to describe the person. After one minute in which the first team get as many right as they can, the first member of the next team then has a go at getting her team to guess as many names as possible. The game goes on with each chick taking a turn at describing to her team, until all the names in the bag or hat have been used. Scores are totted up and all the names are put back into the bag.

The second round works in the same way, but this time the person doing the describing can only use three words for each name. For example, again if the name is Brad Pitt, she might say, 'Phwoargh! Married Friend.' Again this round goes on with each chick having a turn until all the names have been guessed. The scores are added up and the names returned to the bag.

The final round follows the same pattern but this time each chick must mime the names to her teammates. Watching your mate prancing around after a few glasses of wine impersonating Brad Pitt should provide you all with a bit of entertainment. The game continues with a minute for each team member until all the names are gone. Tot your scores up and see who reigns victorious.

Additional Drinking Rules

To add more drinking rules to your games you will need to nominate a Miss Rules (usually the chief bridesmaid) who can be put in charge of adding new rules throughout the night, such as no pointing, no right-hand drinking and no calling anyone by their first name. Here are a few suggestions to get you started but, once you get going, you can add pretty much any rule you like.

Lady Thumbs: one chick is declared to be Lady Thumbs. When they put their thumb on the table, other players must copy and put the correct thumb on the table. The last player to do so drinks a two-finger fine and then becomes Lady Thumbs. Also try Lady Foot, Head or Tongue (depending on how agile/hammered/health-conscious you are feeling).

Dancing Queen: one chick is declared to be the Dancing Queen. When they stand up and dance, the other players must do the same.

The last one up drinks a two-finger fine and becomes the Dancing Queen. This obviously goes completely to pot once you get in a nightclub where you will all become Dancing Queens! Other variations include Rock Goddess (the air guitar queen) and Surf Chick (surfing those bar breakers).

Ms Weights and Measures: this person will issue and monitor fines throughout the night (or for as long as she is capable).

Chairwoman: nominate one of your group to issue a fine to anyone who makes an unreasonable request, and also to have final say in any disputes over fines or rules throughout the night.

The Morning After the Night Before

The recipe for a perfect morning after the night before is a hearty brunch (or lunch by the time you all get organised) and a good debrief of the night's activities. Feed your hangovers and dissect every moment. If you can, this is a perfect time to get the photos developed so you can have a laugh at all the gorgeous pictures. Get a copy for each chick to take home as a reminder of a fantastic Alternative Hen night.

We all know the best hangover cure is a gossip over a greasy fry-up, but if that doesn't work, try some of these suggested remedies:

◆ Drink water by the gallon before you go to bed and when you wake up – the old faithful is the best for your shrivelled brain and muscles.

◆ Spread lots of honey or jam on your toast to raise your blood sugar levels or have Marmite to boost your vitamin B reserves.

◆ Eat a banana to replace lost potassium from dehydration.

◆ Ginger or peppermint tea will calm the nausea.

◆ Or try camomile tea to reduce acidity in your stomach.

◆ Or, if all else fails, go back to bed and sleep it off!

Alternative Activities

If you are able to arrange an entire Alternative Hen weekend around the all-important night then you don't have to limit your daytime activities to shopping and lunch. Getting away from your normal routine will make the experience more special and memorable. These ideas, listed alphabetically, will get your imagination flowing and the Alternative Directory at the back of the book will give you some pointers for where to find what you are looking for. We have given each a star rating out of five, based on novelty value, excitement factor and suitability for a hen do.

Amusement Park ★★

If you haven't been to a theme park since you were eight years old then this is a great option as you can revert to being a kid, eat candyfloss all day and make your hen go at the front on all the biggest rides. It might be better to go with a smaller group, otherwise you may end up spending all your time on your mobile trying to find everyone else.

Bungee Jump ★★★★

Arrange for your hen to have her life flash before her eyes as a rite of passage before she enters into the world of marriage. This is an amazingly exhilarating experience none of you will want to miss, and it'll make sure your hen night ahead is pumped up with adrenaline.

Canal Boat Trip ★★★

Whether it's the Norfolk Broads, the Thames or the Grand Union Canal, picture yourselves drifting along the waterways, stopping at all the pubs along the way and sunbathing on deck with a cold beer in your hand. As long as you keep your wits about you as you go through the locks and can remember your Girl Guide sailing knots, this can be a very relaxing way to spend a weekend. For a detailed look at possible canal routes in the UK, check out www.canalboats.co.uk, or www.britishwaterways.co.uk.

Castle or Cottage Weekends ★★★

If you're not into the whole idea of pubbing and clubbing then have a look into renting a cottage or even a castle for the weekend. The cost will come down a lot when you split it between a group of you. Take along a stack of games and a case of red wine and settle in. You can still have a theme and can still spring some forfeits on your hen to keep her at the centre of attention. Look in the back of Sunday supplements or on the Internet for companies and individual owners renting out a whole host of cottages and unique properties. Start with:

www.observercottages.co.uk

www.lakelandcottages.co.uk

www.classic.co.uk

www.ruralretreats.com or www.landmarktrust.co.uk.

Chocolate Tasting ★★★

Mmm, lovely chocolate … Just think of it – big vats of gorgeous velvety chocolate just waiting to be dived into. Back in reality you could spend your day visiting a chocolate factory where you will find out all about your beloved cocoa beans and, more importantly, get to taste lots of samples. For a good starting point, have a look at www.cadburyworld.co.uk, which has details for the Cadbury factory in Bournville. Also for whole trips that revolve around chocolate (imagine it!) have a look at www.visitbelgium.com/chocol.htm.

Circus Skills Day Course ★★★★★

If you've always fancied yourself as a bit of an acrobat then this is certainly a hen weekend with a difference. Swing gracefully on a trapeze, jump around on a trampoline and learn to juggle with more than two balls. Chilli Sauce organises a great day in London, see www.chillisauce.co.uk/active/lazy/index.php.

Clay Pigeon Shooting ★★★★

Pull! If you fancy a bit of country air then don your Barbour jacket and wellies and take to the fields. Clay pigeon shooting is just as suitable for beginners as it is for old-time professionals, so test out your skills. Especially good for those with a bit of a competitive streak.

Comedy Club ★★

For a change to the pub crawl/nightclub routine, book a night at a comedy club so you can heckle the stand-ups. Some clubs serve food and, once the comedians have vacated the stage, many transform into nightclubs so you can shake your stuff on the dance floor. Have a look at www.jongleurs.co.uk and www.thecomedystore.co.uk.

Dance Class ★★★★★

Ask at a dance school or gym in the area whether there is a tutor who would be willing to host a private dance class for you and your chicks in the afternoon. This is particularly relevant if you are having a 'Fame/Flashdance' or 'Spanish Señorita/Salsa' theme as you can ask to be taught a dance routine that you can use later in the night to wow the crowds. Or, if you feel like something a bit more saucy, you can perfect your pole dancing skills at select studios – have a look at www.mypole.co.uk/takelessons.htm for more information.

Flying ★★

Not a particularly sociable activity but this is a major treat for your hen if she has always dreamed of taking to the skies. You can choose from taking a helicopter flight, a flying lesson in a small aircraft or getting to grips with a microlight. See 'Flying' under each town in the directory and call for some advice or, alternatively, have a look at Virgin Experiences for some ideas at www.virgin.com/experience.

Hang Gliding ★★★

This involves running to the edge of a sheer drop and keeping on going, while putting all your faith in a large kite to stop you from dropping out of the sky like a stone. Fantastic fun and a few of you can go at once so it's good for a group activity. It doesn't take all day either. If you're going to do this it's wise to take it fairly easy the night before because, although it's definitely exhilarating, all that running and adrenaline won't be great with a hangover.

Horse Racing ★★★

For a group of sophisticated ladies there's nothing like a day at the races. Dust down your best frocks and treat yourselves to tickets to the Members' Enclosure so you can swan around drinking Pimms and ogling all the gorgeous chaps in their suits. For more well-known events, such as Royal Ascot, you will need to buy your tickets well in advance so that you don't miss out. It might leave you broke but you'll have a great day. You will find details for some of the major events of the horseracing calendar under Alternative Events.

Horse Riding ★★

If you don't fancy just watching the horses and want to get a piece of the action then treat yourselves to a gentle trot or bracing gallop across the fields and feel the wind in your hair. It doesn't matter if you haven't been on a horse since that one lesson when you were eight years old – you will be able to find a class to suit all levels of expertise. Also very good for toning up your thighs.

Hot Air Ballooning ★★★

Up, up and away! If you're feeling like a flight of fancy then this is a sophisticated option and a good excuse to crack open the champers early. You can fly in a balloon and enjoy an amazing view over most cities in the UK. Just remember to sit on the bottom of the basket if you're afraid of heights and remember this option can be weather dependent. Better for small groups obviously – you try fitting fifteen squawking chicks in a basket.

Karting ★★★★

A good option for the girl racer hen who wants a bit of action. Many karting tracks will allow you to book as a group and race against each other. Have a spin around the track and let her win of course. If you're lucky you could find somewhere that you can race against a group of stags, so you can show them what you girls are made of.

Limousine Hire ★★

You may feel that a limousine is a 'must-have', whatever theme you are considering, and splitting the cost between a group of you will make it more manageable. That way you can all feel like stars for the night, sipping champagne as you spin around town behind tinted windows. Some companies will even arrange for a red carpet to be put down for you when you arrive at your destination. Have a look on the web for firms who rent out limos to hen parties.

Medieval Banquet ★★

One for the buxom wenches out there. Throw yourselves back in time and enjoy a medieval banquet for the night. Enjoy tankards of mead and a feast fit for King Henry VIII (and his six wives) with merrymaking minstrels to entertain you. Have a look at www.medievalbanquet.com for banquets in London to get an idea of what's involved.

Motor Experience Days ★★★★

If your hen has got a passion for speed and has always harboured a secret desire to be a girl racer then treat her to a day behind the wheel.

This option will be sure to make her stag drool with jealousy. Specialist companies will allow you to get behind the wheel of a Ferrari or Lamborghini or, if you don't think much of your own driving skills, this is worth it just to be spun round the track by a true professional. If you need some inspiration check out www.virgin.com/experience or www.drivingexperiences.co.uk.

Murder Mystery ★

It was Colonel Mustard in the library with the candlestick! You may have a hen who is a budding detective and likes to solve a mystery. If so, consider a murder mystery evening for one of the nights of your weekend. There are companies that arrange functions for the public and also those who will organise an event just for you. Or, if you are looking for a cheap option, you can buy a box set to host a murder mystery party for yourselves. The Internet is a good starting place to find a company in your area – start with www.murdermysteryevents.com or www.murdermostfoul.co.uk.

Outdoor Activities ★★★★

Outdoor activity centres throughout the UK cater for those chicks who want a bit of variety in their lives. They will set up a day of activities for you all to enjoy with anything from archery to abseiling, raft racing to quad biking. The choice of things to do varies from centre to centre but this will certainly get your adrenaline rushing ready for a night on the town.

Outdoor Concerts and Theatre ★★

Sitting out in the sunshine, nibbling sausage rolls and sipping white wine spritzers to the sound of beautiful music. If this sounds like your cup of tea, there are an increasing number of summer concerts held at various stately homes and parks around the UK. These often go on into the night and end with a fireworks finale. Despite the British summer usually being approximately four days long, outdoor theatre is also increasingly popular and you can enjoy a drop of culture watching a Shakespeare play in the afternoon before your very uncultured night on the tiles. Some stately homes are listed in the directory but you could also search the web for outdoor theatre in your area as plays and venues may change from year to year. A starting point for Shakespeare can be found at www.openairshakespeare.com.

Paintballing ★★★★

Looking for a lungful of fresh air and to get your pulse racing? If you want something different and very energetic, paintballing could be a good choice. You get to run around in the woods in camouflage getting splattered with paint for the day and it's even more fun if you're hunting down a team of stags …

Pampering ★★★

This is the traditional choice for hens and it's easy to see why. Treat yourselves to a day of pampering in preparation for the night ahead. Many health clubs have day passes that include the use of the basic facilities such as the sauna and spa. Blatantly ignore signs to the gym and head for the restaurant instead for a long, lazy lunch. Lounge around in fluffy white dressing gowns and spoil yourselves with extra treatments such as a massage or facial. You can club together to buy an additional surprise treatment for your hen, such as a full body massage or a manicure and pedicure so she feels extra special. Prices do vary for some of the more glamorous venues so check how much all your chicks are willing to splash out before you book.

Parachute Jump ★★★★

You want an adrenalin rush? Well, this is a rather pricey way to take a metaphorical leap into married life but one your hen will not forget in a hurry! Realistically, in a day you can only do a tandem jump where, thankfully, you will be strapped to someone who does know what they're doing so you can concentrate on breathing while you free-fall through the skies. Absolutely exhilarating! For more information, see www.tandemjump.co.uk and www.jumpwithus.co.uk.

Picnic ★

If you're a bit short on cash or just feel like some fresh air then pack up an assortment of sumptuous treats for an afternoon picnic in the park, or on the beach or wherever else is suitable. If you're feeling energetic, take a Frisbee or initiate a game of rounders or football (the perfect way to get some lads involved …).

Polo Match ★★★★★

Polo, Pimms and maybe even the odd prince if you're lucky. Have a leisurely afternoon watching a polo match or, if you feel like splashing out, go one better and have a go yourselves. It doesn't matter if you've never ridden before as the horses will know more than you anyway. You will be taught the basics and even get to play a mini-match with trophies and everything! Go to www.polo.co.uk and call for more information. Major fixtures are listed at www.hpa-polo.co.uk but the best games to see are the high-goal matches.

Pottery Painting ★★★

Specialist pottery painting cafés are springing up all over the place and this is a lovely way to while away more hours than you think. You simply choose the item you would like to paint, such as a mug or vase, and then exercise your artistic flair and get painting. Most places have books and a collection of completed pieces to give you a bit of inspiration. If you fancy being a bit cheeky then your hen can be instructed to make something covered in her artistic impression of men's nether regions that she has known and loved. When you're booking, ask if there are any special deals for hen parties as some shops will decorate your table and offer champagne (or at least let you bring a bottle of your own so you can have a glass of bubbly while you paint). Check in the directory or with the local tourist centre to see if there is a pottery painting café in the town you are visiting.

Pub Crawl ★

Not particularly alternative you say, but how about doing the Circle Line pub crawl around London? The rules are simple: you must have a drink in a pub by every Underground stop on the route. Or why not crawl your way around the Monopoly Board? You can adapt this for any town that you are visiting. Not for the faint hearted!

Recording Studio ★★★★

If your hen has always harboured a secret desire to have a top 40 hit then she can be a star for the day as she records her favourite song in a professional recording studio. With the girls providing her backing vocals and a CD to take home, this is a day that will be ringing in your ears for a long time to come (especially if you discover she's tone deaf). Gift experience companies such as www.memorisethis.com can organise this for you.

Sailing ★★★★

Oh a life on the ocean wave. How about a weekend of sailing for you and the girls for a great bonding experience? You don't have to be professional sailors as companies that charter yachts will make sure you have a qualified skipper and mate aboard to show you the ropes. Many companies are to be found on the south coast so, if you book well in advance, you could combine a bit of sailing with a trip to Cowes Week.

Salsa Clubs ★★

Shake those maracas and click your heels for a sultry night learning to salsa and cha-cha-cha. Clubs often hold classes before the regulars turn up to show you how it's done. So shimmy your hips and let a professional take you round the floor. This is a great one to combine with a Spanish señorita theme. For starters, check out www.salsa.co.uk.

Scuba Diving ★

OK, so the waters off the UK are hardly the Great Barrier Reef but your hen may have a thing about the deep blue sea and scuba diving could be something that she has always wanted to try. Many companies will give you a 'trial run' if it's your first time. Or if you all have some experience of diving then you could go on a shipwreck dive for a hen day with a difference. Not for everyone as you will need to pass medical tests to be able to dive.

Singalonga ★★★

Fast becoming a cult favourite, the Singalonga group now tour around the UK with three different shows: The Sound Of Music, Abba and Joseph and the Technicolour Dreamcoat. As the name suggests, you watch the film or show and subtitles are provided to the songs so that you can sing along to your heart's content. The audience get very into the whole thing so you'll find yourself surrounded by Abba look-alikes or virginal Marias. Guaranteed to be a great laugh, even if it is a bit surreal chanting along to 'Doe A Deer' next to a group of nuns. Good for a Friday night. You will find all the information you need at www.singalonga.com.

Skiing and Snowboarding ★★★

Shoop, shooping down a crisp white ski run is another active way to spend your day. And if you're not lucky enough to be able to fly everyone out to Val D'Isere (or if it's mid-summer) then you can ski or snowboard on real snow all year round at the Tamworth Snowdome (www.snowdome.co.uk) or Xscape in Milton Keynes (www.xscape.co.uk). Failing that, artificial ski-slopes can be found near most towns in the UK.

Tenpin Bowling ★

Strike! There isn't really any excuse to sink this low for your hen night but it could kill an hour or two in the afternoon if you really have no other option and have a secret desire to rent out someone else's shoes.

The Dogs ★★★

The hare is oooon the move! It's not just for the boys; a night at the dogs is a great laugh for a group of girls too. Many stadiums have restaurants where you can have a slap-up meal while you watch the race action. Use your expert skills to pick a winner or use the traditional girls' technique of betting on the one whose name you like best.

Water Sports ★★★★★

For all those water babes out there who fancy donning a luminous life jacket for the day, this is the perfect choice. Most centres offer a whole host of water sports to choose from, anything from white-water rafting to water-skiing, windsurfing and sailing. Think about something that all your chicks will enjoy and squeeze into your oh-so-flattering wetsuit. Part of the attraction of spending an invigorating day splashing around is that you can look forward to that refreshing hot shower at the end of the day before you go out on the town.

Wine Tasting ★★

How does a day of quaffing fine wines sound? Well, you don't even have to cross the Channel as, believe it or not, you can actually find vineyards in the UK, so you can imagine you are swanning around in the French countryside for the day. If you think Chardonnay is a character in a tacky TV show then you get twice the pleasure as you can learn something while getting pleasantly tipsy. Many UK vineyards are based in the south of England but have a look at www.english-wine.com to see if there's a vineyard in your area. Or take a short cut and visit London's 'Vinopolis' wine museum (www.vinopolis.co.uk) on the South Bank to sample their fare and then pop down to the riverside pubs for the rest of the day.

Zorbing ★★★

For a truly bizarre experience, strap your hen into a giant inflatable ball and throw her down a hill. No, this isn't because you've had enough of her telling you how gorgeous her fiancé is – this is known as zorbing and, strangely, it is really catching on. The sensation of zorbing is said to be close to feeling weightless. The rest of you can join in by having a go or even by lying in the pathway of the zorb to make your hen's journey down the hill that bit more eventful. Organisers describe the rotational motion of the zorb as 'quite relaxed'. Why not find out for yourselves ... You can even zorb in twos or threes, so don't think you can get out of it! Find out more about zorbing at www.zorbsouth.co.uk.

Alternative Events – Home and Away

JANUARY

Alpine Skiing World Cup, Hahnenkamm Downhill Race – Kitzbuhel, Austria

Kitzbuhel is known as a glamorous ski resort and this event is said to be one of the most thrilling in the ski calendar and the whole town comes alive to celebrate the occasion. Go out early to enjoy a day or two skiing before the professionals get on the slopes and spend the rest of the weekend indulging in fondue and Austrian beer with lots of sporty skiers with very muscular thighs.

Web: www.hahnenkamm.com

Bommel Festival – Ronse, Belgium

The folk of Ronse seize any opportunity to have a party. The main spectacle of this parade are the 'Bommels', characters dressed in enormous costumes whose main aim is to knock each other senseless on a day they have named, not surprisingly, Crazy Monday. This, coupled with the general festive atmosphere and Belgian beer, should make for a good knees-up to warm the winter nights.

Web: www.visitflanders.com

FEBRUARY

Venice Carnival – Venice, Italy

The world famous Venice Carnival turns the streets of the city into a theatrical stage for the ten days leading up to Ash Wednesday each year. Masked performers add glamour and mystery to the masses of partygoers who flock here from all around the world for the occasion. And they wonder why Venice is sinking … You'll need to book accommodation well in advance but the Venice Carnevale will provide an extravagant and dramatic backdrop for your Alternative Hen weekend.

Web: www.venicecarnival.com

Carnaval – Cadiz, Spain

Carnaval is celebrated all across Spain in the week running up to Shrove Tuesday. But Cadiz takes its inspiration from the Venice Carnival and really knows how to throw a party. People travel from miles around to come to this infamous celebration. Fancy dress is the order of the day and the spirit is very much alcohol enriched, further enhancing the great entertainment provided by bands, dancers, the parade and individual street artists. Accommodation gets booked up well in advance, so either get organised a couple of months ahead of time, or resign yourself to travelling in from a nearby town along with many of the other revellers.

Web: www.cadizturismo.com

Cologne Carnival – Cologne, Germany

In the build-up to Ash Wednesday, the whole city kicks off for a week-long festival leading up to three days of 24-hour partying in the Old Town. The Germans show the results of their fine beer-making skills, bands play, everyone seems to get into the spirit by getting into fancy dress, and flirting is the order of the day. It is popular with visitors, but it is nowhere near as touristy as the Munich Oktoberfest. A bunch of girls in fancy dress looking for a good time should fit right in.

Web: www.koeln.de

MARCH

St Patrick's Day – Ireland (and any Irish pub in the world)

Ah, the charming Irish lilt and a velvety pint of Guinness. Dublin is the obvious choice to join in the craic but go into any Irish pub in the world on St Patrick's Day and the celebrations will be in full swing. So, if your hen night falls in March, take advantage. The Americans also go crazy for Paddy's Day. Cities such as New York have a huge population of ex-pats who love to go totally over the top. Or you could check out Chicago where, not to be outdone, they go to the trouble of dyeing the river green to show their love of the Irish. For a full week of festivities in Dublin check out www.stpatricksday.ie/cms.

Cheltenham National Hunt Festival and Gold Cup – Cheltenham, UK

In mid-March the first of the major events of the horse racing calendar takes place at Cheltenham. The festival runs from the first Tuesday of the month each year, with visitors coming from all over the world to enjoy the races. You will have to extend your hen weekend into more of a hen week, but that just gives you an excuse to make your celebrations last longer.

Web: www.cheltenham.co.uk

Glasgow International Comedy Festival – Glasgow, Scotland

Not as well known as its big brother festival in Edinburgh in August but that means that there are fewer crowds, less hype and less price hiking too. Glasgow is a really underrated city in the UK – in the past it's been named the City of Culture for Europe, and it has a great nightlife and activities to offer a group of chicks. The comedy festival attracts a lot of the usual favourites on the circuit and also provides a forum for budding talent.

Web: www.glasgowcomedyfestival.com

Ivrea Orange Festival – Ivrea, Italy

Not as well known as the Spanish tomato throwing extravaganza but along similar lines as the people of Ivrea take to the streets and throw oranges at each other in honour of their town's traditions. Intriguing if nothing else and the locals are very passionate about it. You can even be made an honorary citizen of Ivrea for the day so that you can join in with one of the orange-throwing teams. After all that physical exertion the festivities culminate in a bonfire centrepiece in the town square with copious amounts of alcohol to fuel the party mood.

Web: www.carnevalediivrea.it/defaulteng.shtm

Las Fallas – Valencia, Spain

Over two million people make their way to this great Spanish festival each year. Every neighbourhood sponsors the creation of a massive papier-mâché sculpture, called a 'fallas'. These can take up to a year to build and are erected overnight on street corners so that on 15 March, the town awakes to a surreal exhibit of huge, magnificent caricatures of Spanish celebrities and figures from local culture. So the likelihood is that you won't know who any of them are, but that shouldn't make a difference to your overall enjoyment. The partying goes on for days, with the highlight being incredible nightly fireworks displays where neighbourhoods compete for who can make the most noise. Definitely one to head for if you want a riotous hen weekend.

Web: www.fallas.com (only in Spanish) or www.turisvalencia.es

Eurochocolate – Rome, Italy

Not to be outdone by the Chocolate Show in New York in November, Eurochocolate dedicates an entire week to the sweet treat. The festival takes place in Rome every March and is the stuff of dreams for a group of chocoholics. Everywhere you look there is something to do with chocolate, but the highlight is undoubtedly a gigantic chocolate egg that weighs over five and a half tonnes; take a moment to imagine it …
Combine a visit with seeing a few other Roman sites and this could be the perfect weekend for a group of girls.

Web: www.eurochocolate.roma.it (only in Italian)

APRIL

Grand National – Aintree Racecourse, UK

You'll need to book your tickets well in advance for the Grand National as it is undoubtedly one of the highlights of the racing year and tickets for some enclosures sell out months before. The lead up to the race goes on for three days but the buzz on the day is not to be missed. Noise around the course reaches fever pitch as the Grand National race approaches. As if that wasn't enough, bands and live acts entertain the crowds from dawn till dusk to make this a fantastic day out all round.

Web: www.aintree.co.uk/website/index.html

Oxford–Cambridge Boat Race – London, UK

This legendary boat race takes place every April on the River Thames as Oxford and Cambridge battle it out year after year. Quite apart from the excitement of cheering on the rowers (and appreciating their fine muscular form) the route of the race is perfect for a pub crawl along the river, which is particularly good if the sun is shining. Check out the website below so you can decide which pub to sit outside while you watch the race and then plan your route for descending into drunkenness throughout the afternoon.

Web: www.theboatrace.org

Queen's Day – Amsterdam, The Netherlands

If your hen night falls in April and you thought Amsterdam was a party city on any other day of the year, you should combine your celebrations with Queen's Day. Usually around the last weekend of April, the festival is laid on for the Queen's official birthday, and it keeps her very popular indeed. The canals are jammed with boats cruising the waterways, albeit it very slowly, and the streets are packed with a real carnival atmosphere. The city's squares and parks play host to stages for free music concerts, and beer and food is sold at the kerbside. Everyone gets completely slaughtered (the Dutch being one of the few nationalities to rival the Brits in terms of drinking) and, amazingly, there's rarely any trouble. Although, that could be down to the other local produce on offer. To top it all off, the Dutch show their true colours by all dressing in orange and fancy dress for the day, so choose your theme and join the party.

Web: www.visitamsterdam.nl

Jazz and Heritage Festival – New Orleans, USA

A bit further afield but N'Awlins, as the locals call it, is the city of cooool. Infamous for its chilled vibe, jazz, Cajun food, sexy dancing, paddle steamers on the Mississippi and southern-style hospitality, the city plays host to Jazzfest, running for two weekends every spring. Nice. Stages all over town host acts from traditional jazz, to blues, folk, gospel and electric jazz to name but a few. Again, you'll need to book in advance because the festival is now attracting about half a million visitors, and becoming more popular and diverse every year. Also be sure to try the local 'Hurricane' cocktail delicacy while you're there – just the one will do as it is lethal!

Web: www.nojazzfest.com

MAY

FA Cup Weekend – Cardiff Millennium Stadium

For football-loving girls this is one of the main events of the sports year and a lively way to kick off your hen weekend. The final is hosted at the magnificent Cardiff Millennium Stadium, so you can combine a trip to watch the match with a night out in this vibrant city.

Web: www.thefa.com or www.cardiff-stadium.co.uk

Bantry Mussels Festival – Bantry, Ireland

Ideal for a hen weekend that's chilled out with lots of good humour, food and drink. The folk of Bantry have taken the local delicacy and combined it with the national pint to form the basis of the Bantry Bay Mussels Festival – that is mussels and stout. Free mussels are available in every pub and café and before you've taken your first bite, you're bound to find a pint of stout in your hand. You might as well wave goodbye to your stomach for the next few days! If you feel like you need to recover then you can always get some bracing fresh air in the beautiful Irish hills before going back for more.

Web: www.bantrymusselfair.ie

Cat Laughs Comedy Festival – Kilkenny, Ireland

A good alternative to Dublin and home of a great pint, Kilkenny now hosts a celebrated comedy festival bringing together popular comedians and fresh faces from the Irish and UK circuits. Brewery tours at Murphy's are an optional extra.

Web: www.thecatlaughs.com or www.kilkenny.ie

JUNE

Wimbledon Lawn Tennis Championships – Wimbledon, London, UK

Wimbledon is unquestionably the number one event of the tennis calendar and a beloved British institution. Strawberries and champagne are an absolute must to get in the mood for a day on centre court. Unfortunately tickets for this event are pretty much like gold dust. You've got to be pretty keen on tennis to queue up from dawn to even get into the grounds but if you've got what it takes (and can persuade your mates that it's a good idea) this is a great day out for the girls.

Web: www.wimbledon.org

Royal Ascot – Ascot, UK

This is the horse racing event of the year to be seen at, so get your best frock on for the occasion. Racegoers are just as concerned with what they are wearing as they are with the racing itself. Make sure you buy your tickets well in advance for the Members' Enclosure, then you can sit back with your Pimms and binoculars to ogle all the men in their fancy suits.

Web: www.ascot.co.uk

Glastonbury Festival – Pilton, UK

Synonymous with mud and tents as far as the eye can see but Glastonbury has a charm all of its own and attracts major headlining acts year after year. If you're a dab hand with a tent pole then pitch up and settle in for the weekend, but if you don't fancy that you can just go for a day and enjoy the festivities.

Web: www.glastonburyfestivals.co.uk

Epsom Derby – Epsom Downs, UK

They say it's the sport of kings but it's just as much fun for a group of chicks. Epsom is a big one in the racing calendar and the crowds gather from early in the morning. You can pay to be in the grandstand or the Members' Enclosure but the view is just as good from the middle of the course where you can lay out a picnic and place your bets with the numerous bookies. There are also loads of food stands and a music stage for added entertainment, so this makes a fantastic day out before the night ahead.

Web: www.epsomderby.co.uk

Roskilde Festival – Roskilde, Denmark

If you fancy going to a music festival with the girls and want to get out of the UK, Europe's biggest and, reputedly, best rock music festival takes place at the end of June or beginning of July every year just outside Copenhagen. Profits are given to initiatives for youth projects or humanitarian work, and the event attracts major headline acts. In the past this has included traditional rock bands such as Metallica, Iron Maiden and Nirvana. It's not all long hair and mosh pits as even the likes of Coldplay and Bob Marley have been featured on the line-up.

Web: www.roskilde-festival.co.uk

JULY

Henley Royal Regatta – Henley, UK

You don't need to be a water sports fanatic to attend the Henley Royal Regatta. A group of chicks can have a gorgeous day by the river, eating a huge picnic lunch and cracking open a few bottles of Pimms in the sunshine. This event is quintessentially British, with men in boaters and ladies in frocks, and has a real garden party feel about it.

Web: www.hrr.co.uk

Running of the Bulls – Pamplona, Spain

This world famous event is part of the Fiesta de San Fermín that takes place every July in Pamplona. The bull runs take place at eight every morning and hundreds of locals and tourists take to the streets to try to outrun them, which can be pretty hair-raising at the best of times, but a hundred times worse if you've got a hangover from the night before, so perhaps it is best left to the experienced. Anyway, if you don't really fancy running for your life there is plenty to do besides. Be prepared, sleep deprivation is par for the course with fireworks and partying every night and a marching band waking up the town at dawn.

Web: www.pamplona.net

Schlagermove – Hamburg, Germany

A veritable feast of kitsch, this street festival pays homage to German retro-pop and 70s classics. Over 700,000 partygoers don their flares and turn out for this event every year so it must be doing something right. The perfect way to enhance a cheesy 70s theme and live out your Eurovision fantasies all in one go.

Web: www.schlagermove.de

Bastille Day – Paris, France

Embrace the ideals of *liberté*, *egalité* and *fraternité* with our French neighbours as they mark the storming of the Bastille. The perfect excuse to combine your hen festivities with a weekend in Paris as every café, restaurant and club will be holding its own celebrations. Not to mention the endless partying in the streets with the focus on the Champs Elysées and a finale of a fantastic fireworks display at the Trocadéro. The ideal place for a group of chicks looking for a party.

Web: www.franceguide.com

Love Parade – Berlin, Germany

If you're into dance music then this is the event for you as it is the biggest party of its kind and has an international reputation. Endless vibrant floats wind their way around the city with almost one and a half million revellers dancing alongside. It is billed as a celebration of love and freedom so it fits in perfectly with the sentiment of a hen's last night of liberty!

Web: www.loveparade.net

Witnness Festival – Dublin, Ireland

If you are looking for an excuse to head for Dublin, Witnness is fast becoming a highlight of the Irish music calendar. It takes place at the Fairyhouse Racecourse and entices some big-name acts across the Irish Sea every year. The local tipple obviously plays a big part in the revelry and, as with many festivals, you can settle in for the weekend and camp out under the stars.

Web: www.witnness.com

Ollesummer – Tallinn, Estonia

This is an increasingly popular destination for stags so there is no reason why hens shouldn't join in the fun. Tallinn hosts the Baltic region's biggest beer festival at the beginning of July each year, attracting crowds from all over the neighbouring countries, not forgetting local celebs. Not that you'll recognise any of them, but who cares as the beer will be flowing and you'll be caught up in a singalong with the locals in no time.
Web: www.ollesummer.ee

AUGUST

Cowes Week – Isle of Wight, UK

Hello, sailor … Even if you're not sailing, Cowes Week makes for an exciting spectacle. While the boats are racing, the atmosphere on dry land is carnival-like with street performers and live bands to entertain you. There are plenty of bars and cafés to choose from to have a cold beer in the sun while you plan your activities for the night ahead.
Web: www.cowesweek.co.uk

Great Tomato Fight – Buñol, Spain

If you harbour a secret desire to get into a massive food fight, the annual Tomatina will allow you to live out your fantasies. The fiesta kicks off with a week of parades, fireworks, music and dancing to mark a historic food fight of yesteryear. On the day of the great tomato war, 20,000 locals and tourists take to the streets to pelt each other with 125,000 kilos of ripe tomatoes. The main sparring event lasts for just over an hour before the local fire department arrives to dowse everyone off, so a spare set of clothes is a wise move. Then it's back to the local bars and restaurants in great spirits to swap stories on your chucking prowess over a glass of sangria.

Web: www.pilot.co.uk/festivals/Tomatina.html

Notting Hill Carnival – London, UK

For the course of three days over August Bank Holiday weekend the Notting Hill area of London is buzzing with the world famous Notting Hill Carnival. West Indian, African, Asian and European cultures all mingle together in a riot of colour, sequins and feathers in a seemingly endless street parade. The pavements are packed with carnival goers soaking up the sun and supping up their beers. A group of gals in fancy dress with a drink in hand will fit right in! Great fun, but not ideal for a large group as you'll find it difficult to stay together in the swarm of revellers.

Web: www.mynottinghill.co.uk/nottinghilltv/carnival-facts.htm

Birdman Competition – Bognor Regis, UK

If you like to be beside the seaside then why not combine it with a trip to see the annual Birdman competition in Bognor Regis. Every year competitors construct elaborate bird costumes and 'flying' machines and throw themselves off the end of the pier to see who can jump/fly the furthest. Some even start their jump with a run up 'routine'. Definitely a high potential for hilarity, so sit back in your deckchairs with your ice creams and watch this bizarre spectacle unfold.

Web: www.birdman.org.uk

Edinburgh Festival – Edinburgh, Scotland

Every street and building in every part of the city comes alive during the Edinburgh Festival. There are endless plays, comedy shows and concerts to see every hour of every day with loads of up-and-coming and established acts. The festival runs concurrently with the jazz, book, fringe and film festivals and the Military Tattoo, so, as you can imagine, the city is heaving and one of the most exciting places to be at the end of summer. Combine this with a buzzing nightlife and a weekend at the Edinburgh Festival can't fail to be a hit for your hen.

Web: www.eif.co.uk or www.edfringe.com

V2 Music Festival – Chelmsford and Staffordshire, UK

Something in August that's not on the bank holiday weekend! This festival is held the weekend before and is two-centred with one event in Chelmsford and another in Stafford. Bands quite often appear at both on different days. And this attracts the big acts too, with names such as Coldplay and the Red Hot Chilli Peppers featuring. Make a weekend out of it or, alternatively, just go for the day and then arrange something else for a varied hen weekend.

Web: www.vfestival.com

Mathew Street Festival – Liverpool, UK

Liverpool combines International Beatles Week (cue 60s fancy dress theme) with the largest city-centre music festival in the UK. Over 250,000 revellers roam the streets to watch bands performing on six stages around the city. Street performers are also out in the force to entertain the crowds. A good one to combine with a hen weekend as all the entertainment is free.

Web: www.mathewstreetfestival.com

Creamfields – Liverpool, UK

If you're more into dance music, this is one of the key events of the year. Creamfields brings together a host of talented DJs and bands such as the likes of Faithless and Underworld. Held at the old Liverpool Airport, it is getting bigger year on year. From just a dance event with a number of arenas, Creamfields now features fairground rides, a swimming pool and the legendary five-a-side football. Fun in the sun for one day only, so you can combine it with more activities in and around Liverpool to make a full weekend of it.

Web: www.cream.co.uk/creamfields

SEPTEMBER

Oktoberfest – Munich, Germany

Although named Oktoberfest, this world famous festival runs from the end of September for two weeks each year. Six million litres of beer are consumed each year, which gives you a pretty good idea of what the festival consists of. But there is more: with music and parades to entertain the crowds, the whole of Munich gets in party mood. So find a brewery tent to suit your taste and raise a plastic glass – *Prost*!

Web: www.oktoberfest.de

Northern Lights – Lapland

For a very special hen weekend for girls who want to do something truly unique, fly up to Lapland to witness the phenomenon of the Northern Lights, a spectacular natural light show that you will never forget. There is a complicated scientific reason why this display occurs, which you will learn about while you are there, but it is enough just to experience this amazing natural phenomenon.

Web: www.laplandfinland.com

OCTOBER

Jeneverfeesten – Hasselt, Belgium

Belgium may be famous for its beer, chocolates and waffles but in October the folk of Hasselt display their hidden talent and play host to their very own gin festival. So if you are into your G&Ts you can enjoy the samples on a tour of one of the local distilleries and there's even a fountain that offers free-flowing gin. Somebody pass the tonic!

Web: www.visitflanders.com

Goose Fair – Nottingham, UK

OK, so it's basically a fairground but Nottingham Goose Fair is one of Europe's largest, with more than 150 rides and 450 games to entertain you. Not really worth a special trip but if you are having your hen weekend in Nottingham anyway then it's worth dropping by for a toffee apple and a quick spin on the waltzer.

Web: www.nottinghamgoosefair.co.uk

Italian Job Rally – Imola, Italy

You can't get a much more Alternative Hen experience than taking part in the *Italian Job* Rally. This homage to the classic Michael Caine movie takes place every year for charity and is billed as 'an adventure of a lifetime with a difference and a real purpose'. You have to be the proud owner of a Mini (or any other car that is featured in the film) to be eligible for entry but you will be joining 100 like-minded, Mini-loving enthusiasts. The event takes place in Imola and then you will drive back in convoy through amazing European scenery. If you can gather together a group of girls who are up for it (and your hen can get time off before her wedding and honeymoon), this adventure will have your stags drooling with envy!

Web: www.italianjob.com

NOVEMBER

Berlin Jazz Festival – Berlin, Germany

If you're a jazz lover then you can't get much better than JazzFest Berlin to feed your desires. This is one of the most important European festivals in the 'jazz calendar' with concerts in assorted venues around Berlin. A Fringe Jazz Festival runs alongside the main event so the city is alive with entertainment for four days.

Web: www.berlinerfestspiele.de

Biggest Liar in the World Competition – Wasdale, Cumbria, UK

Once a year in the cold, miserable month of November, the Santon Bridge Inn of Wasdale in Cumbria tries to find the Biggest Liar in the

World. The event has been going for over a quarter of a century and was inspired by a local landlord who was renowned for his far-fetched statements. Entrants must try to convince judges that they are naturally gifted liars and regale listeners with obscure and bizarre stories. All very entertaining and to top it off Wasdale is a beautiful part of the Lakes to visit. So, even though the weather may be against you, you can get some time on the hills to stretch those legs. It'll make that glass of wine in front of a roaring fire all the sweeter.

Web: www.santonbridgeinn.com/liar and www.golakes.co.uk

The Chocolate Show – New York, USA

Chocoholics take note … imagine a whole exhibition devoted to chocolate! It's almost too much. You can learn all about the history of chocolate, how it is made and the etiquette surrounding it. More importantly, there are plenty of samples to try and different types of chocolate to buy. Indulge for the day but you can also combine this with a whole weekend enjoying the Big Apple, so get your bucks ready for some serious shopping with the girls.

Web: www.chocolateshow.com

DECEMBER

Open-air Ice-skating – Somerset House, London, UK

Jayne Torvill will get a run for her money when you step out on to the rink to enjoy the open-air skating at Somerset House. All very Christmassy and snuggly for a winter's night with the girls and if you are struggling on your skates you can always take a seat and enjoy a glass of mulled wine while you watch. The rink is in place from November through till January each Christmas but is very popular, so book in advance.

Web: www.somerset-house.org.uk

Edinburgh Hogmanay – Edinburgh, Scotland

New Year's Eve with bells on. Hogmanay takes the celebrations to new extremes with major bands playing on stages in the street, fireworks and a huge bonfire. And, as you'd expect, it is incredibly popular, with more than 500,000 people attending every year – so advance bookings are a must, especially for a large group. Also, it is unlikely that your hen is going to want to spend her New Year's Eve away from her future husband so this is one to consider if you are planning a shag/hag party at this time of year for the two of them.

Web: www.edinburghshogmanay.org

The Icehotel – Kiruna, Swedish Lapland

Every year, the Icehotel is designed and then fashioned from the heavy snowfall in Lapland. Even when visitors are staying, there is constant embellishment going on. From the hotel to a replica of Shakespeare's Globe, all adorned with ice sculptures, the buildings are magnificent. Furs are used to give warmth in the guest rooms. And then, every spring, the elaborate structures melt in the thaw to be built again the following year.

Web: www.arctic-experience.co.uk or www.visit-sweden.com

International Ideas

Look online and you'll find that cheap flights are widely available these days as the budget airlines are all competing for your business.

Check out:

Air Berlin (www.airberlin.com)

BMI Baby (www.bmibaby.com)

easyJet (www.easyjet.com)

Fly.be (www.flybe.com)

MyTravelLite (www.mytravellite.com)

Ryanair (www.ryanair.com)

and Virgin Express (www.virginexpress.com).

Amsterdam

Tourist information: www.visitamsterdam.nl or www.simplyamsterdam.nl

Hen potential: although this is a traditional haunt for stag nights, Amsterdam has lots to offer hens too, with an exciting nightlife and a great relaxed atmosphere. Most Amsterdam folk get around by bicycle so cycle along the tree-lined canals in convoy and visit the museums and art galleries in the day. Make sure you take a rest in one of the many pavement cafés and save some energy for Amsterdam's thriving nightlife.

Barcelona

Tourist information: www.barcelonaturisme.com

or www.simplygoingaround.com/barcelona

Hen potential: there is culture galore to be explored in this city: gaze at the gorgeous Gaudi buildings and admire Picasso's early works; wander down La Rambla and soak up the lively atmosphere before flamenco-ing the night away.

Berlin

Tourist information: www.btm.de or

www.simplygoingaround.com/berlin

Hen potential: a weekend in Berlin is a little piece of history, with splendid restored buildings and museums to explore. The cutting-edge nightlife here has an excellent reputation and the locals are heavily into their dance music. They also, bizarrely enough, have a name for themselves as great tango dancers.

Budapest

Tourist information: www.budapestinfo.hu

Hen potential: fly to Budapest to get a bit further away from the norm.

Fewer people speak English, which can make things more interesting! This is a city famous for its abundance of thermal spas, so you can relax in a totally different environment and also sample the up-and-coming Hungarian wines.

Copenhagen

Tourist information: www.woco.dk

Hen potential: you may have to apply for a bank loan before you leave home but Copenhagen is another alternative option for hens. The summer is the perfect time to be here with lots of open-air music and street performances to be enjoyed. Make your way to the famous Tivoli Park for a day of play before dressing up for a night out on the Danish tiles.

Dublin

Tourist information: www.visitdublin.com or www.simplygoingaround.com/dublin

Hen potential: an abundance of Irish accents, pints of blissful Guinness and the infamous '*craic*', what more could you want for your hen night? Dublin boasts magnificent Georgian buildings, plenty of open green space right in the city centre and a relentless nightlife. Book your accommodation well in advance for this extremely popular city, especially around St Patrick's Day.

Ibiza

Tourist information: www.ibiza-spotlight.com

Hen potential: the well-known clubbing capital has more to offer than just the infamous nightlife, with great beaches, water sports and even a spot of sightseeing; although cheap cocktails and all-night revelry are a good enough reason to visit the island. More importantly, you'll be able to top-up your tan for the wedding.

Las Vegas

Tourist information: www.lasvegas.com

Hen potential: if you're all feeling a bit flash with your cash then wing your way to Las Vegas for a weekend of glitz and glamour on the strip. Enter the surreal casino world of no clocks, no windows, all you can eat and free drinks. Just don't get too carried away and end up marrying Elvis in the drive-thru chapel.

Madrid

Tourist information: www.aboutmadrid.com

Hen potential: from the dramatic Main Square to the stunning parks and gardens, Madrid is an outdoor city best explored on foot – except for in the insane heat of the summer when you're better off in a bar drinking ice-cold sangria. Santa Ana is the most popular place to stay and is perfect for access to all the good nightclubs and restaurants.

Munich

Tourist information: www.munich-tourist.de

Hen potential: beer, beer and more beer ... Munich is home to the world famous crazy Oktoberfest but this city does have more to offer and is bursting with culture, if that is what you are looking for. Indulge in the café culture, street performances and nightlife; Munich is definitely a place that knows how to have a good time.

New York

Tourist information: www.nyctourist.com or www.nycvisit.com

Hen potential: the Big Apple has a unique buzz that will make your adrenaline rush and, if you're a shopaholic, your bank balance plummet. After a night in the sassy bars and clubs, plan a posh brunch à la *Sex and The City* to dissect every detail.

Paris

Tourist information: www.visit-paris.com or www.thingstodo-paris.com

Hen potential: strolling along the Seine, sitting in pavement cafés and feasting on gorgeous French cuisine, Paris is famous as a romantic cliché but also has a lot to offer a group of girls looking for a good time (not least the accents of those foxy Frenchmen). If you've only got time for a fleeting visit, get yourselves 'Nightclubber' Eurostar tickets and dance the night away in Parisian style before catching the first train back in time for breakfast.

Prague

Tourist information: www.praguetourist.com or www.visitprague.cz

Hen potential: already a favoured stag destination but hens should enjoy a piece of Prague too as it is stunningly beautiful and also compact so you will be able to pack a lot into a weekend. There's plenty to entertain you, from the culture of museums and Gothic architecture to lively bars and clubs. Also, perhaps more importantly for a hen party, the beer is delicious and very, very cheap.

Reykjavik

Tourist information: www.tourist.reykjavik.is or www.reykjavik.com

Hen potential: definitely an Alternative Hen night and although everything is more expensive than in the UK, Reykjavik is one of the most popular non-budget destinations for Brits. It's clear to see why – the city is surrounded by breathtaking scenery, has an ultra-cool nightlife and numerous thermal spas to relax your hen ready for her big day. Also, for a truly unforgettable experience, coincide your trip with the natural phenomenon of the Northern Lights. Remember that in the height of the tourist season in summer, Reykjavik has a midnight sun, which means there is no night, whereas in the depths of winter there are only two hours of half-light in an otherwise dark day.

Verona

Tourist information: www.tourism.verona.it

Hen potential: more of a calm, cosy option for a girls' weekend away and certainly not for the more outrageous hen, but this city offers beautiful architecture, gorgeous Italian food and wine and an opera festival in the summer in the stunning amphitheatre. Verona is perfect to explore on foot and the locals enjoy promenading along the streets. You can even pretend to be Juliet on the very balcony that Shakespeare wrote about.

Warsaw

Tourist information: www.warsaw-travel.com or www.warsaw1.net

Hen potential: not necessarily for a wild night out but for a cultural weekend with a difference visit this stunning city. The Old Town was rebuilt from scratch after the devastation of World War II and this fact alone will make you marvel at the beauty of it. You will find plenty of clubs and bars as in any other city but open-air cafés and art exhibitions also abound, so this is a perfect choice for a calmer hen who wants something a bit unique.

Essentials

It's easy to forget the little things when you've got so much to plan so here's a list of those essentials for your Alternative Hen night.

◆ Forfeits written on cards in little envelopes (you can buy these from any good stationer) – keep them hidden from your hen till the moment is right to take her by surprise.

◆ Bad old photos of hen for your props.

◆ Dodgy photos of past boyfriends for speeches or a keepsake book.

◆ Those essential sparkly false eyelashes and wig.

◆ Home-made placemats with cringe-worthy photos of your hen.

◆ Willy novelties for your straws – you'll find these (and lots more besides) in Ann Summers.

◆ Disposable cameras – take a couple of these and snap away at every opportunity, then develop a film for every chick to take away.

◆ Games – plan which ones you would like to play in advance so you have any necessary props ready.

◆ Keepsake/presents for your hen.

◆ Sparklers, balloons and streamers to enhance the party atmosphere!

To Do Checklist

The list below will help you get organised in the weeks leading up to your big night out.

Three months before

☐ Get together your list of invitees and co-ordinate your diaries to see when everyone is free so that you can set the date.

☐ Check with your hen whether she has a burning desire to go anywhere in particular.

☐ Check the Alternative Events listings to see if there is anything that takes your fancy.

☐ Book accommodation for everyone – you may need to book this further in advance if you are thinking of renting a cottage, especially in the summertime.

Two months before

☐ Choose your theme (remember to try to keep it as a surprise for your hen).

☐ Book your transport (if you are not driving) to take advantage of advance fare offers.

One month before

☐ Decide on your outfits and plan what your hen will wear.

☐ List any props that you will need and start buying these as you see them.

☐ Book your daytime activity (you may need to do this further in advance if it is something that will get booked up).

☐ Make a reservation for your group at your chosen restaurant.

Two weeks before

☐ Check if you can get on the guest list at your chosen nightclub to save queuing, explain you are a hen party and many places will give you a free bottle of 'champagne' – take a reference name or number so that you can confirm your booking if necessary.

One week before

☐ Confirm your daytime activity booking.

☐ Confirm your accommodation booking.

☐ Make sure you have all you need for your outfits (including the outfit for your hen).

☐ Buy any last-minute props that you need.

The day before

☐ Confirm that everyone knows where and when to meet.

☐ Check you've got enough camera film to last the night/weekend.

☐ Stock up on any hangover cures that you will need the morning after.

☐ Confirm your restaurant reservation and take a note of who takes your booking for reference on the night.

☐ Let everyone know if they owe you any money so far so that they are prepared.

The night

☐ Check you've got your camera, money and props ready.

☐ Get a kitty together to pay for rounds of drinks and the meal – this will save any hassle with splitting the bill.

☐ Keep your all-important forfeit cards handy to spring on your hen.

Essential Tunes

If you're driving to your destination make a tape or CD to play on your way there to get everyone in the mood. Put together a personalised mix for your hen of tracks she loves, songs from your teenage years or classic hen party tunes so you can sing your hearts out as you head off down the motorway. Here are just a few of the many girly tracks you could include:

◆ Ladies Night – Kool & The Gang

◆ Lady Marmalade – LaBelle

◆ Groove Is In The Heart – Deee Lite

◆ Dancing Queen – Abba

◆ Girls Just Wanna Have Fun – Cyndi Lauper

◆ It's Raining Men – The Weather Girls

◆ We Are Family – Sister Sledge

◆ A Night To Remember – Shalamar

◆ I'm Every Woman – Chaka Khan

Shags and Hags

If you've made it to thirty without getting hitched, you may prefer the idea of a shag or a hag. Don't worry, it's not as bad as it sounds … If the hen and stag are best buddies and he's an integral part of your group of mates, you could arrange a night or a weekend away that also includes him and your shared mates.

The themes, games and activities in this book still stand and there's also an *Alternative Stag* book, which might help to find the right middle ground for a shag party. Just bear in mind the old 'what the eye doesn't see' rule, i.e. don't get the stag and hen to do the more flirtatious challenges if it's likely to end up in a bar brawl.

When it comes to daytime fun, anything that lends itself to a 'lads versus lasses' competition is ideal. Top activities suited to mixed groups include:

- canal boats;
- castle or cottage;
- circus school;
- clay pigeon shooting;
- It's a Knockout;
- karting;
- outdoor activities;
- white-water rafting.

Tailor-made Hen Nights

Finally, if you just don't have the time or the inclination to plan your festivities, let someone do it all for you. These companies will take it all out of your hands:

Chilli Sauce
Telephone: 0845 450 7450
Web: www.chillisauce.co.uk

Crocodile Events
Telephone: 0115 911 5758
Web: www.crocodileevents.co.uk

Eclipse Leisure
Telephone: 0870 2000 6969
Web: www.eclipseleisure.com

Great Escapades
Telephone: 0870 010 0505
Web: www.great-escapades.org

Great Weekends
Telephone: 0845 450 4333
Web: www.great-weekends.co.uk

Last Night of Freedom
Telephone: 0870 751 4433
Web: www.lastnightoffreedom.co.uk

Organize Events
Telephone: 0845 330 3940
Web: www.organize-events.co.uk

Playaway Weekends
Telephone: 01225 350 075
Web: www.playawayweekends.com

Red Seven Leisure
Telephone: 0870 751 7377
Web: www.henparty.co.uk

Suggested Accommodation

Hotel chains are good for booking accommodation for groups but if you fancy something a bit more personal contact the local tourist information centre for a list of options.

Best Western
Telephone: 08457 747474
Web: www.bestwestern.co.uk

Thistle Hotels
Telephone: 0870 333 9292
Web: www.thistlehotels.co.uk

De Vere Hotels
Telephone: 0870 606 3606
Web: www.devereonline.co.uk

Travel Inn
Telephone: 0870 242 8000
Web: www.travelinn.co.uk

Holiday Inn
Telephone: 0870 400 8161
Web: www.holidayinn.co.uk

Travel Lodge
Telephone: 0870 085 0950
Web: www.travelodge.co.uk

Alternative Directory

This directory will give you a starting point for activities in a selection of cities around the UK. They are listed in alphabetical order and will help you to plan where to go and what to do for your Alternative Hen night.

Listings under Outdoor Activity Centres include: 4 x 4 driving, abseiling, archery, blindfold driving, canyoning, clay pigeon shooting, climbing, gorge walking, Honda pilots, hovercraft, It's a Knockout, mud buggies, quad biking, raft racing, ropes courses.

Under Watersports (and some Outdoor Activity Centres) you will find: canoeing, jet-skiing, kayaking, powerboating, sailing, surfing, wakeboarding, waterskiing, windsurfing.

Avoid disappointment

When you are choosing which nightclub to go to, it goes without saying that you will need to check whether there is a dress code. And it's worth trying to get on the guest list so you don't have to queue.

And be sure to have a look at the 'More Alternative Activities' section at the end for even more unique ideas.

This isn't a watertight list and you should make sure that the listing you choose fits the style and budget you're looking for. If you can't find what you are after, call up the local tourist information centre or have a browse around the Internet.

BATH

Bath Tourist Information Centre
Abbey Chambers, Abbey Church Yard, Bath BA1 1LY
Telephone: 0906 711 2000
Email: tourism@bathnes.gov.uk
Web: www.visitbath.co.uk or www.bath.info

Comedy Clubs
See Bristol listings.

Flying
Bath, Wilts & North Dorset Gliding Club
The Park, Kingston Deverill
Warminster BA12 7HS
Telephone: 01985 844095
Web: www.bwnd.co.uk

Golf
Bath Approach Golf Course (pitch & putt)
Victoria Park, Bath BA1 2NR
Telephone: 01225 331162
Web: www.bathpublicgolf.co.uk

Entry Hill Golf Club
Entry Hill, Bath BA2 5NA
Telephone: 01225 834248
Web: www.bathpublicgolf.co.uk

Combe Grove Manor Driving Range
Brassknocker Hill, Monkton Combe
Bath BA15 7HS
Telephone: 01225 835533
Web: www.combegrovemanor.com

Horse Racing
Bath Racecourse
Lansdown, Bath BA1 9BU
Telephone: 01225 424609
Web: www.bath-racecourse.co.uk

Horse Riding
See High Action under Outdoor Activity Centres
for Bristol.

Hot Air Ballooning
Balloons Over Bath
Greenacre Lodge, Breadstone, Berkeley GL13 9HF
Telephone: 01453 810018
Web: www.balloonsoverbath.co.uk

Bath Balloon Flights
8 Lambridge, London Road, Bath BA1 6BJ
Telephone: 01225 466888
Web: www.balnet.co.uk

First Flight (Central Bath)
Telephone: 01225 484060
Web: www.firstflight.co.uk

Karting
Castle Combe Kart Track
Castle Combe Circuit, Chippenham SN14 7EX
Telephone: 01249 783010
Web: www.combe-events.co.uk

Nightclubs
Cadillacs
90B Walcot Street, Bath BA1 5BG
Telephone: 01225 464241

PoNaNa
North Parade, Bath BA2 4AL
Telephone: 01225 401115
Web: www.ponana.co.uk

Babylon
Kingston Road, Bath BA1 1PQ
Telephone: 01225 400404
Web: www.ponana.co.uk

Outdoor Activity Centres
See High Action under Outdoor Activity Centres
for Bristol.

Pursuits
33 Reybridge, Lacock, Chippenham SN15 2PF
Telephone: 01249 730388
Activities: archery, blindfold driving, clay pigeon
shooting, quad biking

Mill On The Brue
Trendle Farm, Bruton BA10 0BA
Telephone: 01749 812307
Web: www.millonthebrue.co.uk
Activities: abseiling, archery, canoeing, clay pigeon
shooting, climbing, grass skiing, grass toboggans,
jet skiing, quad biking, raft racing, zip wire

Combe Grove Manor Hotel & Country Club
Brassknocker Hill, Monkton Combe
Bath BA2 7HS
Telephone: 01225 835533
Web: www.combegrovemanor.com
Activities: archery, casino evenings, clay pigeon
shooting, It's a Knockout, murder mystery, quad
biking, reverse steer car races, themed barge
nights

Paintball
See Bristol listings.

Pampering
The Bath Spa Hotel
Sydney Road, Bath BA2 6JF
Telephone: 0870 400 8222
Web: www.bathspahotel.com

Combe Grove Manor Hotel & Country Club
Brassknocker Hill, Monkton Combe, Bath BA2 7HS
Telephone: 01225 835533
Web: www.combegrovemanor.com

Lucknam Park Leisure Spa
Colerne, Chippenham, Wiltshire SN14 8AZ
Telephone: 01225 740537
Web: www.lucknampark.co.uk

The Cow Shed
Babington House, Babington, Nr Frome
Somerset BA11 3RW
Telephone: 01373 813860
Web: www.babingtonhouse.co.uk

Scuba Diving
Bath Dive Centre
Upper Bristol Road, 1 Cork Place, Bath BA1 3BB
Telephone: 01225 482081
Web: www.bathdivecentre.co.uk

Skiing & Snowboarding
See High Action under Outdoor Activity Centres
for Bristol.

Watersports
Cotswold Water Park
Keynes Country Park, Shorncote
Cirencester GL7 6DF
Telephone: 01285 861459
Web: www.waterpark.org

BELFAST

Belfast Welcome Centre
47 Donegall Place, Belfast BT1 5AD
Telephone: 02890 246609
Email: belfastwelcomecentre@nitic.net
Web: www.gotobelfast.com

Flying
Ulster Flying Club
Ards Airport, Portaferry Road
Newtownards BT23 8SG
Telephone: 02891 813327
Web: www.ulsterflyingclub.com

Golf

Mount Ober Driving Range
24 Ballymaconaghy Road, Knockbracken BT8 6SB
Telephone: 02890 795666

Craigavon Golf Centre
Turmoya Lane, Silverwood, Lurgan BT66 6NG
Telephone: 02838 326606
Web: www.craigavonboroughcouncil.gov.uk

Horse Racing

Down Royal Racecourse
Maze, Lisburn BT27 5RW
Telephone: 02892 621256
Web: www.downroyal.com

Horse Riding

Lagan Valley Equestrian Centre
170 Upper Malone Rd, Dunmurry
Belfast BT17 9JZ
Telephone: 02890 614853

Karting

Formula Karting
Greenbank Business Centre
Warrenpoint Road, Newry BT34 2QX
Telephone: 02830 266220
Web: www.formula-karting.com

Ultimate Karting
11 Kilbride Road, Doagh, Ballyclare BT39 0QA
Telephone: 02893 342777
Web: www.ultimatekarting.com

Nightclubs

Benedicts
7–21 Bradbury Place, Belfast BT7 1RQ
Telephone: 02890 591999
Web: www.benedictshotel.co.uk

Robinsons
38–42 Great Victoria Street, Belfast BT2 7BA
Telephone: 02890 247447
Web: www.belfastpubs-n-clubs.com

Empire Bar
42 Botanic Avenue, Belfast BT7 1JQ
Telephone: 02890 249276
Web: www.belfastpubs-n-clubs.com

M-Club
23–31 Bradbury Place, Belfast BT7 1RR
Telephone: 02890 233131
Web: www.belfastpubs-n-clubs.com

Outdoor Activity Centres

Corporate Solutions
Lower Knockbarragh Road, Rostrevor BT34 3DP
Telephone: 02841 739333
Web: www.eastcoastadventure.com
or www.corporate.ie
Activities: abseiling, banana skiing, clay pigeon
shooting, deep sea fishing, golf, helicopter flights,
horse riding, jet skiing, powerboats, rock climbing,
yachting

Protosport
61 Mullantine Road, Portadown BT62 4EJ
Telephone: 02838 331919
Web: www.protosport.co.uk
Activities: karting, off-road buggies, quad biking

Paintball

Escarmouche Paintball
Unit 5, 19 Donegall Pass, Belfast BT7 1DR
Telephone: 02890 327500
Web: www.escarmouche.com

Pampering
Impressions Health & Beauty Clinic
(Aromatherapy & Reflexology)
Burrendale Hotel, Castlewellan Road
Newcastle Co. Down BT33 0JY
Telephone: 02843 724448
Web: www.impressionshealthandbeauty.com

LivingWell Health Club
Hilton Belfast
4 Lanyon Place, Belfast BT1 3LP
Telephone: 02890 277490
Web: www.livingwell.co.uk

Pottery Painting
All Fired Up Ceramics
190 Cavehill Road, Belfast BT15 5EX
Telephone: 02890 207179
Web: www.allfiredceramics.com

Scuba Diving
Blue Juice Diving
Telephone: 02886 735881
Web: www.bluejuicediving.com
Activities: scuba diving, mountain biking, archery,
paragliding

Skiing & Snowboarding
Craigavon Ski and Golf Centre
Turmoya Lane, Silverwood, Lurgan BT66 6NG
Telephone: 02838 326606
Web: www.craigavonboroughcouncil.gov.uk

Table-side Dancing Clubs
Movie Star Café (lap dancing restaurant for men
& women)
69 Botanic Ave, Belfast BT7 1JL
Telephone: 02890 238643

Tenpin Bowling
Belfast Superbowl
4 Clarence Street West, Bedford Street
Belfast BT2 7GP
Telephone: 02890 331466

The Dogs
Ballyskeagh Greyhound Stadium
New Grosvenor Park, Ballyskeagh Road
Lambeg BT17 9LL
Telephone: 02890 616720

Watersports
Lagan Watersports Centre
2 Rivers Edge, 13–15 Ravenhill Road
Belfast BT6 8DN
Telephone: 02890 461711
Web: www.laganwatersports.co.uk
Activities: canoeing, dragon boating, kayaking,
power boating, rowing, sailing

Craigavon Watersports Centre
1 Lake Road, Craigavon BT64 1AS
Telephone: 02838 342669
Activities: banana boating, canoeing, dragon
boating, kayaking, sailing, wake boarding, water
skiing, windsurfing

BIRMINGHAM

Tourist Information Centre
2 City Arcade, Birmingham B2 4TX
Telephone: 0121 202 5099
Web: www.beinbirmingham.com or
www.marketingbirmingham.com

Casinos
Grosvenor Casino
263 Broad Street, Birmingham B1 2HF
Telephone: 0121 631 3535
Web: www.rank.com

Gala Casino
Hill Street, Birmingham B5 4AH
Telephone: 0121 643 1777
Web: www.galacasinos.co.uk

Comedy Clubs
Jongleurs
Quayside Tower
259/262 Broad Street, Birmingham B1 2HF
Telephone: 0870 240 5721
Web: www.jongleurs.co.uk

Flying
Avon Flying School
Wellesbourne-Mountford Airfield
Wellesbourne CV35 9EU
Telephone: 01789 470727
Web: www.avonflyingschool.com

Flightworks (Midlands) Ltd
Rowley Road, Coventry CV3 4FR
Telephone: 02476 511100
Web: www.flightworks.co.uk

Golf
Cocks Moors Woods Golf Course
Alcester Road South, Kings Heath
Birmingham B14 4ER
Telephone: 0121 464 3584
Web: www.birmingham.gov.uk

Hilltop Golf Course
Park Lane, Handsworth B21 8LJ
Telephone: 0121 554 4463
Web: www.birmingham.gov.uk

Hatchford Brook Golf Centre
Coventry Road, Sheldon B26 3PY
Telephone: 0121 743 9821
Web: www.birmingham.gov.uk

Horse Racing
Warwick Racecourse
Hampton Street, Warwick CV34 6HN
Telephone: 01926 491553
Web: www.warwickracecourse.co.uk

Horse Riding
Hole Farm Trekking Centre
Woodgate Valley Country Park
36 Watery Lane, Quinton B32 3BS
Telephone: 0121 422 3464

Cottage Farm Riding Stables
100 Ilshaw Heath Rd, Warings Green
Hockley Heath B94 6DL
Telephone: 01564 703314

Hot Air Ballooning
Balloons Over The Midlands
Greenacre Lodge, Breadstone, Berkeley GL13 9HF
Telephone: 01453 810018
Web: www.balloonsoverthemidlands.co.uk

Indoor Activity Centres
The Birmingham Indoor Climbing Centre, The
Rockface
A.B. Row, Off Jennens Road, Millennium Point
Birmingham B4 7QT
Telephone: 0121 359 6419
Web: www.rockface.co.uk
Activities: abseiling, caving, climbing, blind
winetasting, rope bridges and other challenges

Karting
Grand Prix Karting
Birmingham Wheels Park, Adderley Road South
Birmingham B8 1AD
Telephone: 0121 327 7617
Web: www.grandprixkarting.co.uk

Nightclubs

Brannigans
200–209 Broad Street, Birmingham B15 1AY
Telephone: 0121 616 1888

Zanzibar
Hurst Street, Birmingham B5 4AS
Telephone: 0121 643 4715
Web: www.zanzibar.co.uk

Tiger Tiger
Five Ways, Broad Street, Birmingham B15 1AY
Telephone: 0121 643 9722
Web: www.tigertiger.co.uk

Outdoor Activity Centres

The Ackers
Golden Hillock Road, Sparkbook B11 2PY
Telephone: 0121 772 5111
Web: www.theackers.co.uk
Activities: abseiling, archery, bowboats, canoeing, climbing, kayaking, orienteering, skiing, snowboarding

Wolverhampton Clay Target Club
Telephone: 01902 790992
Web: www.lesplantshooting.co.uk
Activities: clay pigeon shooting

Paintball

National Paintball Fields (Bassetts Pole)
Metro Triangle, Mount Street, Nechells
Birmingham B7 5QT
Telephone: 0800 358 3959
Web: www.nationalpaintballfields.com

SAS Paintball
Woodhall Farm, Wood Road
Codsall Wood WV8 1QS
Telephone: 01902 844467
Web: www.saspaintball.com

Pampering

The Beauty Salon
Living Well Birmingham Premier
42/44 Priory Queensway, Birmingham B4 7LA
Telephone: 0121 236 7789
Web: www.livingwell.co.uk

Erdington Swimming Pool and Turkish Suite
Mason Road, Erdington, Birmingham B24 9EJ
Telephone: 0121 464 0520
Web: www.leisure.birmingham.gov.uk

Eden Hall Day Spa
Elston Village, Newark
Nottinghamshire NG23 5PG
Telephone: 01636 525555
Web: www.edenhallspa.co.uk

Pottery Painting

Café Ceramica
Mitchell's Art and Craft Centre
Weeford Road, Sutton Coldfield B75 6NA
Telephone: 0121 308 3984
Web: www.cafeceramica.com

Scuba Diving

Scuba Sport
15 Whitminster Avenue, Birmingham B24 9NG
Telephone: 0121 384 5595
Web: www.scubasport.co.uk

Skiing & Snowboarding

The Snowdome
Leisure Island, River Drive, Tamworth B79 7ND
Telephone: 0870 500 0011
Web: www.snowdome.co.uk

Also see The Ackers under Outdoor Activity Centres.

Tenpin Bowling
Megabowl
Pershore Street, Birmingham B5 4RW
Telephone: 0121 666 7525
Web: www.megabowl.co.uk

The Dogs
Hall Green Track
York Road, Hall Green B28 8LQ
Telephone: 0870 840 7400
Web: www.hallgreenstadium.co.uk

Watersports
Hydro Extreme
Action Sports Centre, Worcester Road
Holt, Worcester WR6 6NH
Telephone: 01905 620044
Web: www.hydroextreme.com

H20 Sports
202 Saltwells Road, Dudley DY2 0BL
Telephone: 01384 633984
Web: www.h2osports.co.uk

BLACKPOOL

Tourist Information Centre
1 Clifton Street, Blackpool FY1 1LY
Telephone: 01253 478222
Email: tourism@blackpool.gov.uk
Web: www.blackpooltourism.com

Casinos
Grosvenor Casino
Sandcastle, South Promenade, Blackpool FY4 1BB
Telephone: 01253 341222
Web: www.rank.com

Flying
Blackpool Pleasure Flights
Blackpool Air Centre, Blackpool Airport FY4 2QS
Telephone: 01253 341871

Golf
Stanley Park Municipal Golf Course
Telephone: 01253 395349
Web: www.blackpool.gov.uk

Horse Racing
Haydock Park Racecourse
Newton-Le-Willows WA12 0HQ
Telephone: 01942 402624
Web: www.haydock-park.com

Hot Air Ballooing
Balloons Over Blackburn
Greenacre Lodge, Breadstone, Berkeley GL13 9HF
Telephone: 01453 810018
Web: www.balloonsoverblackburn.co.uk

Karting
Karting 2000
New South Promenade, Blackpool FY4 1TB
Telephone: 01253 406340
Web: www.karting2000.com

Kapitol Karting
275–289 Central Drive, Blackpool FY1 5HZ
Telephone: 01253 292600
Web: www.kapitolkarting.co.uk

Nightclubs
The Syndicate
Church Street, Blackpool FY1 3PR
Telephone: 01253 753222
Web: www.thesyndicate.org

The Waterfront
168–170 North Promenade, Blackpool FY1 1RE
Telephone: 01253 292900
Web: www.ukcn.com

Heaven and Hell
Bank Hey Street, Blackpool FY1 4QZ
Telephone: 01253 625118
Web: www.heavenandhell.co.uk

Outdoor Activity Centres

Adrenalin Zone
South Pier, Promenade, Blackpool FY4 1BB
Telephone: 01253 292029
Web: www.blackpoollive.com
Activities: reverse bungee jump, roller coasters

Adventure 21
21 Babylon Lane, Anderton, Chorley PR6 9NR
Telephone: 01257 474467
Web: www.adventure21.co.uk
Activities: aquaseiling, abseiling, canoeing, caving, canyoning, climbing, culvert scrambling, gorge scrambling, kayaking, mountain biking, orienteering, raft building, windsurfing

A6 Clay Target Centre
Reeves House Farm, Fourgates, Westhoughton
Bolton BL5 3LY
Telephone: 01942 843578
Web: www.a6ctc.co.uk
Activities: clay pigeon shooting

Paintball

Sudden Impact Paintball
Whyndyke Farm, Preston New Road
Blackpool FY4 4XQ
Telephone: 01253 313163
Web: www.sudden-impact.co.uk

Tenpin Bowling

Premier Bowl
Mecca Buildings, Central Drive, Blackpool FY1 5HZ
Telephone: 01253 295503
Web: www.premierbowlblackpool.com

BOURNEMOUTH

The Visitor Information Bureau
Westover Road, Bournemouth BH1 2BU
Telephone: 0906 802 0234 (calls charged at 60p per minute)
Email: info@bournemouth.gov.uk
Web: www.bournemouth.co.uk

Casinos

Gala Casinos
Westover Road, Bournemouth BH1 2BZ
Telephone: 01202 553790
Web: www.galacasinos.co.uk

Comedy Clubs

Check with the Visitor Information Bureau for comedy nights.

Flying

Bournemouth Flying Club
Aviation Park East, Off Matchams Lane
Bournemouth International Airport
Christchurch BH23 6NE
Telephone: 01202 578558
Web: www.bournemouthflyingclub.co.uk

Flying Frenzy Paragliding
1 Mill Terrace, Burton Bradstock
Bridport DT6 4QY
Telephone: 01308 897909
Web: www.flyingfrenzy.com

Golf

Meyrick Park Golf Course
Central Drive, Bournemouth BH2 6LH
Telephone: 01202 786040
Web: www.clubhaus.com

Horse Racing
The Bibury Club Ltd
Salisbury Racecourse, Netherhampton
Salisbury SP2 8PN
Telephone: 01722 326461
Web: www.salisburyracecourse.co.uk

Horse Riding
Sandford Park Riding Stables
Sandford Holiday Park, Holton Heath
Poole BH16 6JZ
Telephone: 01202 621782

Hot Air Ballooning
British School of Ballooning
Little London, Ebernoe, Nr Petworth GU28 9LF
Telephone: 01428 707307
Web: www.hotair.co.uk

Balloons Over Dorset
Greenacre Lodge, Breadstone, Berkeley GL13 9HF
Telephone: 01453 810018
Web: www.balloonsoverdorset.co.uk

Karting
Southern Counties Karting
Wardon Hill, Nr Dorchester DT2 9PW
Telephone: 01935 83666
Web: www.southern-counties.com

Nightclubs
Jumpin Jaks
The Waterfront, Pier Approach
Bournemouth BH2 5AA
Telephone: 07000 311311
Web: www.jumpinjaks.co.uk

Bumbles
45 Poole Hill, Bournemouth BH2 5PW
Telephone: 01202 557006

Berlins
Hinton Road, Bournemouth BH1 2EN
Telephone: 01202 554034
Web: www.berlinsnightclub.com

Bar Med
The Quadrant Centre, St Peter's Road
Bournemouth BH1 2AB
Telephone: 01202 299537
Web: www.bar-med.com

The Great Escape Late Night Bar
176 Old Christchurch Road
Bournemouth BH1 1NU
Telephone: 01202 298866
Web: www.greatescape.uk.com

Outdoor Activity Centres
Henley Hillbillies
Old Henley Farm, Buckland Newton
Dorchester DT2 7BL
Telephone: 01300 345293
Web: www.henleyhillbillies.co.uk
Activities: archery, clay pigeon shooting,
crossbows, hovercraft, mini mavriks, quad biking

Brenscombe Outdoor Centre
Studland Road, Corfe Castle, Dorset BH20 5JG
Telephone: 01929 481222
Web: www.brenscombeoutdoor.co.uk
Activities: abseiling, archery, canoeing, climbing,
horseriding, kayaking, laser clay shooting,
mountain biking, powerboating, quad biking, raft
building, ropes course, survival skills, waterskiing,
windsurfing

Matchams Leisure Park
Hurne Road, Matchams, Nr Ringwood BH24 2BT
Telephone: 01425 473305
Web: www.ringwoodraceway.com
Activities: archery, clay pigeon shooting, karting,
quad biking

Gorcombe Entertainments
Gorcombe Farm, Thornicombe
Nr Blandford DT11 9AG
Telephone: 01258 452219
Web: www.gorcombe.co.uk
Activities: clay pigeon shooting, paintballing,
quad biking

Wessex Sporting Events
624 Hillbutts, Wimborne BH21 4DS
Telephone: 0800 093 3530
Web: www.wessexsportingevents.com
Activities: archery, clay pigeon, Honda pilots,
hovercrafts, paintballing, quad biking

Southern Counties Shooting
Wardon Hill, Nr Dorchester DT2 9PW
Telephone: 01935 83625
Web: www.southern-counties.com
Activities: clay pigeon shooting

Paintball
Master Blaster Paintball
39/4 Merryfield Park, Derritt Lane
Bransgore BH23 7AU
Telephone: 01202 201761
Web: www.bournemouth-paintball.co.uk

Challenge Paintball & Quad Bikes
248 Ringwood Road
St Leonards, Ringwood BH24 2SB
Telephone: 01202 877899

Pampering
Marriott Leisure Club
St Michaels Road, West Cliff
Bournemouth BH2 5DU
Telephone: 01202 294527

The Durley Hall Hotel
Durley Chine Road, Bournemouth BH2 5JS
Telephone: 01202 753305
Web: www.durleyhall.co.uk

De Vere Royal Bath
Bath Road, Bournemouth BH1 2EW
Telephone: 01202 555555
Web: www.devereonline.co.uk

Scuba Diving
Divers Down (Swanage Ltd)
The Pier, Swanage BH19 2AN
Telephone: 01929 423565
Web: www.diversdown.tv

Skiing & Snowboarding
Christchurch Ski Centre
Matchams Lane, Hurn, Christchurch BH23 6AW
Telephone: 01202 499155
Web: www.christchurch-skicentre.com

Tenpin Bowling
Superbowl
Glen Fern Road, Bournemouth BH1 2LZ
Telephone: 01202 291717
Web: www.megabowl.co.uk

The Dogs
Poole Stadium
Wimborne Road, Poole BH15 2BP
Telephone: 01202 677449
Web: www.poolegreyhounds.com

Watersports
Harbour Boardsailing
284 Sandbanks Road, Lilliput, Poole BH14 8HU
Telephone: 01202 700503
Web: www.pooleharbour.co.uk
Activities: windsurfing, kitesurfing

Hengistbury Head Centre
Broadway, Southbourne BH6 4EN
Telephone: 01202 425173
Activities: canoeing, kayaking, low ropes, sailing

Rockley Watersports
Rockley Point, Poole BH15 4RW
Telephone: 01202 677272
Web: www.rockleywatersports.com
Activities: sailing, powerboating, windsurfing

French Connection Watersports
4 Banks Road, Sandbanks, Poole BH13 7QB
Telephone: 01202 707757
Web: www.fcwatersports.co.uk
Activities: kitesurfing, windsurfing, wake boarding

Sail UK
29 Lulworth Avenue, Hanworthy, Poole BH15 4DQ
Telephone: 01202 668410
Web: www.sailuk.net

BRIGHTON

Tourist Information Centre
10 Bartholomew Square, Brighton BN1 1JS
Telephone: 0906 711 2255 (premium rate line, calls cost 50p per minute)
Email: brighton-tourism@brighton-hove.gov.uk
Web: www.visitbrighton.com

Casinos
Grosvenor Casino
9 Grand Junction Road, Brighton BN1 1PP
Telephone: 01273 326514
Web: www.rank.com

Comedy Clubs
Check out www.whatson.brighton.co.uk for listings.

Flying
Sussex Hang Gliding & Paragliding
Tollgate, Nr Lewes BN8 6JZ
Telephone: 01273 858170
Web: www.sussexhgpg.co.uk

Elite Helicopters
Hanger 3, Goodwood Airfield
Chichester PO18 0PH
Telephone: 01243 530165
Web: www.elitehelicopters.co.uk

Airbase Flying Club
The Old Customs Hall
Terminal Building, Shoreham Airport
Shoreham-by-Sea BN43 5FF
Telephone: 01273 455532
Web: www.airbaseflyingclub.co.uk

Golf
Brighton and Hove Golf Club
Devils Dyke Road, Brighton BN1 8YT
Telephone: 01273 556482

Horse Racing
Brighton Racecourse
Freshfield Road, Brighton BN2 9XZ
Telephone: 01273 603580
Web: www.brighton-racecourse.co.uk

Fontwell Racecourse
Fontwell, Arundel BN18 0SX
Telephone: 01243 543335
Web: www.fontwellpark.co.uk

Horse Riding
Beauport Park Riding School
Hastings Road, St Leonards-on-Sea TN38 8EA
Telephone: 01424 851424

Rottingdean Riding School
Chailey Avenue, Rottingdean BN2 7GH
Telephone: 01273 302155

Hot Air Ballooning

British School of Ballooning
Little London, Ebernoe, Nr Petworth GU28 9LF
Telephone: 01428 707307
Web: www.hotair.co.uk

Balloons Over Sussex
Greenacre Lodge, Breadstone, Berkeley GL13 9HF
Telephone: 01453 810018
Web: www.balloonsoversussex.co.uk

Karting

Trax Indoor Karting
46 Brampton Road, Hampden Park Industrial
Estate, Eastbourne BN22 9AJ
Telephone: 01323 521133
Web: www.traxkarting.co.uk

Nightclubs

Babylon Lounge
Western Esplanade, Kingsway, Hove BN3 4FA
Telephone: 01273 207100

Creation
78 West Street, Brighton BN1 2RA
Telephone: 01273 321628
Web: www.applebelly.com

The Beach
171–181 Kings Road Arches, Brighton BN1 1NB
Telephone: 01273 722272
Web: www.thebeachbrighton.co.uk

The Brighton Gloucester
27 Gloucester Place, Brighton BN1 4AA
Telephone: 01273 688011
Web: www.thebrightongloucester.co.uk

Zap
189–192 Kings Road Arches, Brighton BN1 1NB
Telephone: 01273 202407
Web: www.thezapbrighton.co.uk

Outdoor Activity Centres

Madtrax Mudmania
Home Farm, Staplefield
Nr Haywards Heath RH17 6AP
Telephone: 01444 456441
Web: www.mudmania.co.uk
Activities: mudbuggies

Adventure Connections
Shelldale House, 3–9 Shelldale Road
Portslade BN41 1LE
Telephone: 01273 417007
Web: www.adventureconnections.co.uk
Activities: 4 x 4 driving, ballooning, banana boats,
canoeing, clay pigeon shooting, dinghy sailing,
flight simulator, flying, gliding, golf, hovercraft, jet
skiing, karting, murder mystery, off-road karting,
paintballing, paragliding, pleasure flights,
powerboating, power karts, power turns, quad
biking, scuba diving, tank driving, water skiing,
windsurfing, yacht sailing

Blackwool Farm
Colhook Common, Petworth GU28 9ND
Telephone: 01428 707258
Web: www.blackwoolfarm.co.uk
Activities: archery, clay pigeon shooting, fly-
fishing, hot air ballooning, karting, quad biking,
reverse steer driving

Q Leisure
London Road, Albourne, Hassocks BN6 9BQ
Telephone: 01273 834403
Web: www.qleisure.co.uk
Activities: 4 x 4 driving, archery, clay pigeon
shooting, karting, quad biking

Paintball

Demolition Paintball
28 Sompting Avenue (office), Broadwater
Worthing BN14 8HN
Telephone: 01273 418263
Web: www.demolitionpaintball.co.uk

Shootout Paintball
Old Barn Farm, Cinderford Lane
Hellingly, Hailsham BN27 4HL
Telephone: 01424 777779
Web: www.shootout.uk.com

Pampering

The Treatment Rooms
21 New Road, Brighton BN1 1XA
Telephone: 01273 818444
Web: www.thetreatmentrooms.co.uk

Saks Hair & Beauty @ David Lloyd
Brighton Marina, Brighton BN2 5UF
Telephone: 01273 666426
Web: www.sakshairandbeauty.com

Pottery Painting

Paint Pots
39 Trafalgar Street, Brighton BN1 4ED
Telephone: 01273 696682

The Painting Pottery Café
31 North Road, Brighton, BN1 1YB
Telephone: 01273 628952
Web: www.paintingpotterycafe.co.uk

Scuba Diving

Sunstar Diving
160 South Street, Lancing BN15 8AU
Telephone: 01903 767224
Web: www.sunstardiving.co.uk

Skiing & Snowboarding

Knockhatch Ski Centre
Hempstead Lane, Hailsham BN27 3PR
Telephone: 01323 843344
Web: www.knockhatch.com

Tenpin Bowling

Bowlplex
Brighton Marina BN2 5UF
Telephone: 01273 818180
Web: www.bowlplexuk.com

The Dogs

Coral Brighton and Hove Greyhound Stadium
Neville Road, Hove BN3 7BZ
Telephone: 01273 204601
Web: www.coral.co.uk

Watersports

Hove Lagoon Watersports
Hove Lagoon, Kingsway, Hove BN3 4LX
Telephone: 01273 424842
Web: www.hovelagoon.co.uk

The Brighton Kayak Company
185 Kings Road Arches, Brighton BN1 1NB
Telephone: 01273 323160
Web: www.thebrightonkayak.co.uk

Winetasting

Brighton Wine School
9 Foundary Street, Brighton BN1 4AT
Telephone: 01273 672525
Web: www.brightonwineschool.co.uk

BRISTOL

Tourist Information Centre
The Annexe, Wildscreen Walk, Harbourside
Bristol BS1 5DB
Telephone: 0117 926 0767
Email: ticharbourside@bristol-city.gov.uk
Web: www.visitbristol.co.uk

Casinos
Gala Casinos
Redcliffe Way, Bristol BS1 6NJ
Telephone: 0117 921 3189
Web: www.galacasinos.co.uk

Grosvenor Casino
266 Anchor Road, Bristol BS1 5TT
Telephone: 0117 929 2932
Web: www.rank.com

Comedy Clubs
Jesters Comedy Club
140–142 Cheltenham Road, Bristol BS6 5RL
Telephone: 0117 909 6655
Web: www.jesterscomedyclub.co.uk

Flying
Bristol Flying Centre
Bristol Airport, Lulsgate BS48 3DP
Telephone: 01275 474501
Web: www.b-f-c.co.uk

Bath, Wilts & North Dorset Gliding Club
The Park, Kingston Deverill, Warminster BA12 7HS
Telephone: 01985 844095
Web: www.bwnd.co.uk

Golf
Stockwood Vale Golf Club
Stockwood Lane, Bristol BS31 2ER
Telephone: 0117 986 6505
Web: www.stockwoodvale.com

Horse Racing
Cheltenham Racecourse
Prestbury Park, Prestbury, Cheltenham GL50 4SH
Telephone: 01242 537642
Web: www.cheltenham.co.uk

Chepstow Racecourse
Chepstow NP16 6BE
Telephone: 01291 622260
Web: www.chepstow-racecourse.co.uk

Horse Riding
See High Action under Outdoor Activity Centres.

Gordano Valley Riding Centre
Moor Lane, Clapton In Gordano, Bristol BS20 7RF
Telephone: 01275 843473

Hot Air Ballooning
Balloons Over Bristol
Greenacre Lodge, Breadstone, Berkeley GL13 9HF
Telephone: 0117 985 9670
Web: www.balloonsoverbristol.co.uk

First Flight
Telephone: 0117 973 1073
Web: www.firstflight.co.uk

Karting
The Raceway
Avonmouth Way, Avonmouth BS11 9YA
Telephone: 0800 376 6111
Web: www.theraceway.co.uk

West Country Karting
Trench Lane, Winterbourne BS36 1RY
Telephone: 01454 202666
Web: www.westcountrykarting.co.uk

Nightclubs

Brannigans
Harbourside, Canons Way, Bristol BS1 5UH
Telephone: 0117 927 7863

Evolution
Waterfront, Canons Road, Bristol BS1 5UH
Telephone: 0117 922 0330

McClusky's
Pithay Building
All Saints Street, Bristol BS1 2LZ
Telephone: 0117 930 0008
Web: www.mccluskys.com

The Works
15 Nelson Street, Bristol BS1 2JY
Telephone: 0117 929 2658
Web: www.applebelly.com

Outdoor Activity Centres

High Action
Lyncombe Drive, Churchill
Nr Somerset BS25 5PQ
Telephone: 01934 852335
Web: www.highaction.co.uk
Activities: 4 x 4 off-road driving, abseiling, archery, climbing, dry slope skiing, horse riding, mountain biking, quad biking, snowboarding

Chepstow Outdoor Activity Centre
Tump Farm, Sedbury, Chepstow NP16 7HN
Telephone: 01291 629901
Web: www.chepstowoutdooractivities.co.uk
Activities: 4 x 4 driving, archery, clay pigeon shooting, paintballing, quad biking, sphere-mania (zorbing)

BHP Inspiring Events
The Old Stables, Box Hedge Farm
Coalpit Heath BS36 2UW
Telephone: 01454 775541
Web: www.stag-hen-party.com
Activities: archery, clay pigeon shooting, Honda pilots, karting, max kats, quad biking, tank driving

T Z Paintball
Weston Lodge Farm, Valley Road, Portishead
Telephone: 01934 416507
Web: www.tzpaintball.co.uk
Activities: clay pigeon shooting, off-road karting, paintballing, quad biking

Bristol Outdoor Pursuits Centre
Common Wood, Huntstrete, Pensford BS39 4NT
Telephone: 0800 980 3980
Web: www.bristoloutdoor.co.uk
Activities: Honda pilots, paintballing, quad biking

Paintball

Paintball Adventures (Brockley Combe)
31 Hopps Road, Kingswood BS15 9QQ
Telephone: 0117 935 3300
Web: www.paintball-adventures.co.uk

Pampering

Holmes Place Redwood Lodge
Beggar Bush Lane, Failand, Bristol BS8 3TG
Telephone: 01275 394554
Web: www.holmesplace.co.uk

Clifton Relaxation Centre
9 All Saints Road, Clifton, Bristol BS8 2JG
Telephone: 0117 970 6616
Web: www.relaxationcentre.co.uk

Bristol Marriott Royal Leisure Club
College Green, Bristol BS1 5TA
Telephone: 0117 930 4992
Web: www.marriotthotels.co.uk

Pottery Painting
Make Your Mark
97 Whiteladies Road, Bristol BS8 2NT
Telephone: 0117 974 4257
Web: www.makeyourmarkbristol.co.uk

Skiing & Snowboarding
See High Action under Outdoor Activity Centres.

Tenpin Bowling
Megabowl
Brunel Way, Ashton Gate, Bristol BS3 2YX
Telephone: 0117 953 8538
Web: www.megabowl.co.uk

Watersports
See Cotswold Water Park under Watersports for
Bath.

CARDIFF

Cardiff Visitor Centre, 16 Wood Street
Cardiff CF10 1ES
Telephone: 02920 227281
Email: visitor@thecardiffinitiative.co.uk
Web: www.cardiffvisitor.info

Casinos
Grosvenor Casino
Greyfriars Road, Cardiff CF10 3AD
Telephone: 02920 342991
Web: www.rank.com

Comedy Clubs
Jongleurs
Units 1 & 5, Ground & 1st Floor
Millennium Plaza, Wood Street, Cardiff CF10 1LA
Telephone: 0870 240 2731
Web: www.jongleurs.co.uk

Golf
Cottrell Park Golf Club
St Nicholas, Cardiff CF5 6SJ
Telephone: 01446 781781
Web: www.cottrell-park.co.uk

Peterstone Lakes Golf Club
Peterstone, Wentlooge, Cardiff CF3 2TN
Telephone: 01633 680075
Web: www.peterstonelakes.com

Horse Racing
Chepstow Racecourse
Chepstow NP16 6BE
Telephone: 01291 622260
Web: www.chepstow-racecourse.co.uk

Hot Air Ballooning
Balloons Over Wales
Greenacre Lodge, Breadstone, Berkeley GL13 9HF
Telephone: 01453 810018
Web: www.balloonsoverwales.co.uk

Karting
South Wales Karting Centre
Llandow Circuit, Llandow Trading Estate
Cowbridge CF71 7PB
Telephone: 01446 795568
Web: www.stathankartclub.com

Nightclubs
Evolution
Atlantic Wharf, Hemmingway Road
Cardiff CF10 4JY
Telephone: 02920 464444

Flares
96 St Mary Street, Cardiff CF10 1DX
Telephone: 02920 235825

Creation
Park Place, Cardiff CF10 3DP
Telephone: 02920 377021
Web: www.applebelly.com

Surfers Nightclub
Millennium Plaza, Wood Street, Cardiff CF10 1LA
Telephone: 02920 377178
Web: www.regentinns.co.uk

Outdoor Activity Centres
Taff Valley Buggy Trail & Activity Centre
Cwrt-y-celyn Farm, Upper Boat
Pontypridd CF37 5BJ
Telephone: 02920 831658
Web: www.adventurewales.co.uk
Activities: 4 x 4 driving, archery, assault courses,
clay pigeon shooting, orienteering, pony trekking,
quad biking

Merlin Adventures
71 Ty Cerrig, Pentwyn, Cardiff CF2 7DQ
Telephone: 02920 549640
Activities: abseiling, caving, gorge scrambling, hill
walking & mountaineering, improvised rafting,
kayaking, open canoeing, rock climbing

See also Taskforce Paintball Games under Paintball.

Paintball
Taskforce Paintball Games
Llanedos Street, Lythans, Cardiff CF5 6BQ
Telephone: 02920 593900
Web: www.taskforcepaintball.co.uk
Activities: archery, falconry, laser clay shooting,
paintballing

Pampering
Healthworks
Village Hotel and Leisure Club
29 Pendwyallt Road, Coryton, Cardiff CF14 7EF
Telephone: 02920 524300
Web: www.villagehotelsonline.co.uk

The St David's Hotel and Spa
Havannah Street, Cardiff Bay CF10 5SD
Telephone: 02920 454045
Web: www.thestdavidshotel.com

Skiing & Snowboarding
Cardiff Ski Centre
Fairwater Road, Cardiff CF5 3JR
Telephone: 02920 561793
Web: www.skicardiff.com

Tenpin Bowling
Megabowl, Newport Road, Cardiff CF23 9AE
Telephone: 02920 461666
Web: www.megabowl.co.uk

Watersports
Ocean Quest Watersports Centre
Unit 7 West Bute Street, Cardiff CF1 6EP
Telephone: 02920 303545
Web: www.ocean-quest.co.uk

Llanishen Sailing Centre
Llanishen Reservoir, Lisvane Road
Llanishen CF4 5SE
Telephone: 02920 761360
Web: www.llanishensc.connectfree.co.uk

EDINBURGH

Tourist Information Office
3 Princes Street, Edinburgh EH2 2QP
Telephone: 0845 225 5121
Email: info@visitscotland.com
Web: www.edinburgh.org

Casinos
Gala Casino
5 South Maybury Road, Edinburgh EH12 8NE
Telephone: 0131 338 4444
Web: www.galacasinos.co.uk

Comedy Clubs
The Stand Comedy Club
5 York Place, Edinburgh EH1 3EB
Telephone: 0131 558 7272
Web: www.thestand.co.uk

Flying
Scotia Helicopters
Cumbernauld Airport, Cumbernauld G68 0HH
Telephone: 01236 780140
Web: www.scotiahelicopters.co.uk

Microlight Scotland
Cumbernauld Airport, Cumbernauld G68 0HH
Telephone: 07979 971301
Web: www.microlightscotland.com

Golf
Kings Acre Golf Course & Academy
Lasswade, Midlothian EH18 1AU
Telephone: 0131 663 3456
Web: www.kings-acregolf.com

Horse Racing
Musselburgh Racecourse
Linkfield Road, Musselburgh EH21 7RG
Telephone: 0131 665 2859
Web: www.musselburgh-racecourse.co.uk

Horse Riding
Pentland Hills Icelandics
Windy Gowl Farm, Carlops, Penicuik EH26 9NL
Telephone: 01968 661095
Web: www.phicelandics.co.uk

Hot Air Ballooning
Balloons Over Scotland
Greenacre Lodge, Breadstone, Berkeley GL13 9HF
Telephone: 01453 810018
Web: www.balloonsoverscotland.co.uk

Karting
Racing Karts
Arrol Square, Livingston EH54 8QZ
Telephone: 01506 410123
Web: www.racingkarts.co.uk

Fastrax Motorsports
Inzievar Oakley
Telephone: 01383 880300
Web: www.fastrax.org

Nightclubs
Revolution
31 Lothian Road, Edinburgh EH1 2DJ
Telephone: 0131 229 7670
Web: www.revolution-edinburgh.co.uk

Subway Nightclub
69 Cowgate, Edinburgh EH1 1JW
Telephone: 0131 225 6766
Web: www.subwayclubs.co.uk

The Basement (late night bar)
10A Broughton Street, Edinburgh EH1 3RH
Telephone: 0131 557 0097
Web: www.thebasement.org.uk

Outdoor Activity Centres
Mavis Hall Park
Humbie, East Lothian EH36 5PL
Telephone: 01875 833733
Web: www.mavishallpark.co.uk
Activities: archery, blindfold driving, clay pigeon
shooting, falconry, Highland games, off-road
driving, quad biking, reverse steer driving

Cluny Clays Activity Centre
Cluny, Kirkcaldy KY2 6QU
Telephone: 01592 720374
Web: www.clunyclays.co.uk
Activities: 9 hole golf course, 27 bay driving range,
archery & air rifle facilities, clay pigeon shooting,
falconry, Honda pilots, quad biking, reverse steer
Land Rover driving

Nae Limits
Tay Terrace, Dunkeld PH8 0AQ
Telephone: 01350 727242
Web: www.naelimits.com
Activities: canyonning, cliff jumping, duckie trips,
gorge crossing, skiing, rap running (forwards
abseiling), river bugs, white-water rafting

Bedlam Event Management
28 Great King Street, Edinburgh EH3 6QH
Telephone: 07000 233526
Web: www.bedlam.co.uk
Activities: 4 x 4 off-road driving, archery, clay
pigeon shooting, Honda pilots, karting,
paintballing, quad biking, rally driving

Paintball
Skirmish Scotland
Gateside Commerce Park, Haddington
East Lothian EH14 3ST
Telephone: 0131 477 9661
Web: www.skirmishscotland.co.uk

Pampering
Vital Health Fitness & Beauty
The Holyrood Hotel, 81 Holyrood Road
Edinburgh EH8 6AE
Telephone: 0131 528 8181
Web: www.holyroodevents.com

Pottery Painting
Doodles Ceramics Workshop
29 Marchmont Crescent, Edinburgh EH9 1HQ
Telephone: 0131 229 1399
Web: www.doodlesscotland.co.uk

Skiing & Snowboarding
Midlothian Ski Centre
Hillend, Edinburgh EH10 7DU
Telephone: 0131 445 4433
Web: www.ski.midlothian.gov.uk

Tenpin Bowling
Megabowl
Fountain Bridge, Dundee Street
Edinburgh EH11 1AW
Telephone: 0870 850 8000
Web: www.megabowl.co.uk

Watersports
Port Edgar Sailing School and Marina
Shore Road, South Queensferry EH30 9SQ
Telephone: 0131 331 3330
Web: www.portedgar.com

Loch Insh Watersports & Skiing Centre
(2hrs from Edinburgh)
Insh Hall, Kincraig PH21 1NU
Telephone: 01540 651272
Web: www.lochinsh.com

GLASGOW

Greater Glasgow & Clyde Valley Tourist Board
11 George Square, Glasgow G2 1DY
Telephone: 0141 204 4480
Web: www.seeglasgow.com

Casinos
Gala Casinos
Various venues around Glasgow.
Web: www.galacasinos.co.uk

Comedy Clubs
Jongleurs
UGC Dev, 11 Renfrew Street, Glasgow G2 3AB
Telephone: 0870 240 3417
Web: www.jongleurs.co.uk

Flying
Glasgow Flying Club
Glasgow International Airport
Walkinshaw Road, Renfrew PA4 9LP
Telephone: 0141 889 4565
Web: www.glasgowflyingclub.com

Scotia Helicopters
Cumbernauld Airport, Cumbernauld G68 0HH
Telephone: 01236 780140
Web: www.scotiahelicopters.co.uk

Microlight Scotland
Cumbernauld Airport, Cumbernauld G68 0HH
Telephone: 07979 971301
Web: www.microlightscotland.com

Golf
Alexandra Golf Course
Alexandra Parade, Glasgow G31 3BS
Telephone: 0141 556 1294

Knightswood Golf Course
Lincoln Avenue, Glasgow G13 3RH
Telephone: 0141 959 6358

Horse Racing
Hamilton Park Racecourse
Bothwell Road, Hamilton ML3 0DW
Telephone: 01698 283806
Website: www.hamilton-park.co.uk

Horse Riding
Ardgowan Riding Centre
Bankfoot, Inverkip, Greenock PA16 0DT
Telephone: 01475 521390
Web: www.ardgowan-riding.co.uk

Hot Air Ballooning
Balloons Over Scotland
Greenacre Lodge, Breadstone, Berkeley GL13 9HF
Telephone: 01453 810018
Web: www.balloonsoverscotland.co.uk

Karting
Scotkart Indoor Racing
Westburn Road, Cambuslang G72 7UD
Telephone: 0141 641 0222
Web: www.scotkart.co.uk

Nightclubs
Lowdown
158–164 Bath Street, Glasgow G2 4TB
Telephone: 0141 331 4060

The Shed
26 Langside Avenue, Shawlands
Glasgow G41 2QS
Telephone: 0141 649 5020
Web: www.shedglasgow.co.uk

Victorias
98 Sauchiehall Street, Glasgow G2 3DE
Telephone: 0141 332 1444
Web: www.victoriasglasgow.com

Outdoor Activity Centres
Active Outdoor Pursuits
Stayamrie, Benston Road, Cumnock KA18 4PJ
Telephone: 01540 673319
Web: www.activeoutdoorpursuits.com
Activities: abseiling, canoeing, canyoning and
gorge walking, hillwalking, mountain biking,
mountaineering, rock climbing, rope courses,
skiing & snowboarding, ski mountaineering,
white-water rafting

See also Nae Limits and Bedlam Event
Management under Outdoor Activity Centres for
Edinburgh.

Paintball
Scottish Paintball Centre
Meiklemosside, Fenwick KA3 6AY
Telephone: 0141 423 9199
Web: www.scottishpaintballcentre.co.uk

Pampering
The Beardmore Spa
Beardmore Street, Clydebank, Glasgow G81 4SA
Telephone: 0141 951 6000

Oshi Spa @ Langs Hotel
2 Port Dundas Place, Glasgow G2 3LD
Telephone: 0141 333 5701
Web: www.langshotels.co.uk

Scuba Diving
Aquatron Dive Centre
30 Stanley Street, Kinning Park G41 1JB
Telephone: 0141 429 7575
Web: www.aquatron.co.uk

Skiing & Snowboarding
Glasgow Bearsden Ski Club
The Mound, Stockiemuir Road, Bearsden G61 3RS
Telephone: 0141 943 1500
Web: www.skibearsden.co.uk

Tenpin Bowling
AMF Bowling
Elliott Street, Glasgow G3 8DZ
Telephone: 0141 248 4478
Web: www.amfbowling.co.uk

The Dogs
Shawfield Greyhound Stadium
Rutherglen Road, Glasgow G73 1SZ
Telephone: 0141 647 4121
Web: www.thedogs.co.uk

Watersports
Galloway Sailing & Watersports Centre
Parton, Loch Ken, Kirkcudbrightshire
Dumfries DG7 3NQ
Telephone: 01644 420626
Web: www.lochken.co.uk

LEEDS

Gateway Yorkshire Leeds Regional Travel & Tourist
Information Centre
Telephone: 0113 242 5242
Email: tourinfo@leeds.gov.uk
Web: www.leeds.gov.uk

Casinos
Gala Casinos
Wellington Bridge Street, Westgate
Leeds LS3 1LW
Telephone: 0113 389 3700
Web: www.galacasinos.co.uk

Grosvenor Casino
Podium Building, Merrion Way, Leeds LS2 8BT
Telephone: 0113 244 8386
Web: www.rank.com

Grosvenor Casino
Moortown Corner House, 343 Harrogate Road
Leeds LS17 6LD
Telephone: 0113 269 5051
Web: www.rank.com

Comedy Clubs
Jongleurs
The Cube, Units 1, 2 & 4, Albion Street
Leeds LS2 8PN
Telephone: 0113 247 1759
Web: www.jongleurs.co.uk

Flying
Airborne Hang Gliding & Paragliding Centre
The Ranch, Hey End Farm, Luddendenfoot
Halifax HX2 6JN
Telephone: 01422 834989
Web: www.airborne.uk.com

Leeds Flying School
Unit 84, Coney Park Estate
Leeds Bradford International Airport
Harrogate Road, Leeds LS19 7XS
Telephone: 0845 166 2506
Web: www.leedsflyingschool.co.uk

Golf
Oulton Park Golf Club
Rothwell Lane, Leeds LS26 8EX
Telephone: 0113 282 3152
Web: www.leeds.gov.uk

Temple Newsam Golf Club
Temple Newsam, Leeds LS15 0NL
Telephone: 0113 264 7362
Web: www.leeds.gov.uk

Roundhay Golf Club
Park Lane, Leeds LS8 2EJ
Telephone: 0113 266 1686
Web: www.leeds.gov.uk

Horse Racing
Wetherby Racecourse
York Road, Wetherby LS22 5EJ
Telephone: 01937 582035
Web: www.wetherbyracing.co.uk

Horse Riding
Yorkshire Riding Centre
Markington, Harrogate HG3 3PD
Telephone: 01765 677207
Web: www.yrc.co.uk

Hot Air Ballooning
Balloons Over Yorkshire
Greenacre Lodge, Breadstone, Berkeley GL13 9HF
Telephone: 01453 810018
Web: www.balloonsoveryorkshire.co.uk

Karting
Pole Position Indoor Karting, Sayner Lane
Leeds LS10 1LS
Telephone: 0113 243 3775
Web: www.polepositionindoorkarting.co.uk

Kart Skill
Riverside Raceway, South Accommodation Road
Hunslet, Leeds LS9 9AS
Telephone: 0113 249 1000
Web: www.kartskill.co.uk

Nightclubs
Bird Cage Nightclub
52–56 Boar Lane, Leeds LS1 5EL
Telephone: 0113 246 7273
Web: www.birdcagelive.com

Baja Beach Club
43A Woodhouse Lane, Leeds LS2 8JT
Telephone: 0113 245 4088
Web: www.bajabeachclub.co.uk

Majestyk & Jumpin Jaks
City Square, Leeds LS1 4DS
Telephone: 0113 242 4333
Web: www.ukcn.com

Bondi Beach
Queens Buildings, City Square, Leeds LS1 4DS
Telephone: 0113 243 4744

Mint Club
8 Harrison Street, Leeds LS1 6PA
Telephone: 0113 244 3168
Web: www.themintclubleeds.co.uk

Heaven and Hell
9 Grand Arcade, Merrion Street, Leeds LS1 6PQ
Telephone: 0113 243 9963
Web: www.heavenandhell.co.uk

Evolution
Cardigan Fields Leisure Park, Kirkstall Road
Leeds LS4 2DG
Telephone: 0113 263 2632

Outdoor Activity Centres
Stagandhenweekend.com
Holme View, Ilkley LS29 9EL
Telephone: 01943 609334
Web: www.stagandhenweekend.com
Activities: abseiling, clay pigeon shooting,
climbing, karting, off-road driving, paintballing,
quad biking, rafting

Banana Chilli
233 Keighley Road, Cowling, Keighley BD22 0AA
Telephone: 01535 637000
Web: www.bananachilli.co.uk
Activities: 4 x 4 driving, abseiling, archery, bungee
jumping, canoeing, caving, clay pigeon shooting,
climbing, gladiators, golf, gorge walking, Honda
pilots, horse riding, hot air ballooning, hovercrafts,
karting, mountain biking, paintballing, quad
biking, rodeo bull, scuba experience, skiing,
snowboarding, sumo, waterskiing, white-water
rafting

North of England Activity Centre
Tinker Lane, Harewood Whin, Rufforth
York YO23 3RR
Telephone: 01904 738120
Web: www.noeac.co.uk
Activities: 4 x 4 off-road driving, archery, clay
pigeon shooting, grass kart racing, quad biking

Paintball
Paintball Commando
Castle Farm, Milnthorpe Lane, Sandal
Wakefield WF2 7JA
Telephone: 01924 252123
Web: www.paintballcommando.co.uk

Pampering
Virgin Spa
Cardigan Fields Development
Kirkstall Road, Leeds LS4 2DJ
Telephone: 0113 224 6632
Web: www.virgincosmetics.com

Thorpe Park Hotel and Spa
1150 Century Way, Thorpe Park, Leeds LS15 8ZB
Telephone: 0113 204 4333
Web: www.shirehotels.co.uk

Zest Health & Beauty Spa
@ Marriott Hollins Hall Hotel
Hollins Hill, Baildon BD17 7QW
Telephone: 01274 534213
Web: www.marriotthotels.co.uk

Healthworks
Village Hotel, 186 Otley Road, Headingly LS16 5PR
Telephone: 0113 203 3507
Web: www.villagehotelsonline.co.uk

Scuba Diving
Bear Divers
3 Stannigley Road, Armley, Leeds LS12 3AP
Telephone: 0113 217 2800
Web: www.beardivers.co.uk

Skiing & Snowboarding
See Sheffield Ski Village under Skiing &
Snowboarding for Sheffield.

Tenpin Bowling
AMF Bowling Leeds
Merrion Centre, Leeds LS2 8BT
Telephone: 0113 245 1781
Web: www.amfbowling.co.uk

The Dogs
Kinsley Greyhound Stadium
96 Wakefield Road, Kinsley, Pontefract WF9 5EH
Telephone: 01977 610946
Web: www.kinsleydogs.co.uk

Watersports
Leeds Sailing, Canoeing & Kayaking Centre
Yeadon Tarn, Leeds, LS19
Telephone: 0113 250 3616
Web: www.leeds.gov.uk

LIVERPOOL

Tourist Information Centre
Atlantic Pavilion, Albert Dock, Liverpool L1 1RG
Telephone: 0906 680 6886 (calls cost 25p per min)
Email: askme@visitliverpool.com
Web: www.visitliverpool.com

Casinos
Grosvenor Casino
76–78 West Derby Road, Liverpool L6 9BY
Telephone: 0151 260 8199
Web: www.rank.com

Comedy Clubs
Rawhide Comedy Club @ Baby Blue
PO Box 23, Liverpool L17 8FR
Telephone: 0151 726 0077
Web: www.rawhidecomedy.com

Flying
See Lancashire Aero Club under Flying for
Manchester.

Golf
Bootle Golf Course
Dunnings Bridge Road, Liverpool L30 2PP
Telephone: 0151 928 1371

Childwall Golf Club
Naylors Road, Liverpool L27 2YB
Telephone: 0151 487 9871

Horse Racing
Aintree Racecourse
Ormskirk Road, Liverpool L9 5AS
Telephone: 0151 522 2929
Web: www.aintree.co.uk

Haydock Park Racecourse
Newton-Le-Willows WA12 0HQ
Telephone: 01942 402624
Web: www.haydock-park.com

Horse Riding
Foxes Riding School
Badgers Rake Lane, Ledsham, Wirral CH66 8PF
Telephone: 0151 339 6797
Web: www.ridingschools.co.uk

Hot Air Ballooning
Balloons Over The Mersey
Greenacre Lodge, Breadstone Berkeley GL13 9HF
Telephone: 01453 810018
Web: www.balloonsoverthemersey.co.uk

Karting
Mersey Karting
Unit 1, Paragon Centre, Piction Road
Wavertree, Liverpool L15 4LP
Telephone: 0151 734 1736
Web: www.merseykarting.co.uk

Nightclubs
Garlands
Telephone: 0151 709 9586
Web: www.garlandsonline.co.uk

Club 051
1 Mount Pleasant, Liverpool L3 5SX
Telephone: 0151 707 8385
Web: www.theclub051.co.uk

Bar-celona
35 Renshaw Street, Liverpool
Telephone: 0151 709 0880
Web: www.bar-celona.co.uk

The Krazyhouse
16 Wood Street, Liverpool L1 4AQ
Telephone: 0151 708 5016
Web: www.thekrazyhouse.co.uk

Outdoor Activity Centres
Adventure 21
21 Babylon Lane, Anderton, Chorley PR6 9NR
Telephone: 01257 474467
Web: www.adventure21.co.uk
Activities: aquaseiling, abseiling, canoeing, caving,
canyoning, climbing, culvert scrambling, gorge
scrambling, kayaking, mountain biking,
orienteering, raft building, windsurfing

Pro Adventure
23 Castle Street, Llangollen LL20 8NY
Telephone: 01978 861912
Web: www.adventureholiday.com
Activities: abseiling, canoeing, canyoning, gorge
walking, kayaking, mountain biking, rock
climbing, white-water rafting

Altcar Clay Pigeon Club
Altcar Range, Hightown, Near Formby
Telephone: 0151 924 5921
Activities: clay pigeon shooting

Paintball
SWAT Paintball Activities
84 Parkside Road, Bebington CH63 7NR
Telephone: 0151 644 1611
Web: www.swatpaintball.co.uk

Paintball Zone (Knowsley)
46 Garthdale Road, Liverpool L18 5HW
Telephone: 0151 735 0011
Web: www.paintballzone.co.uk

Pampering
The Works
39 Allerton Road, Woolton, Liverpool L25 7RE
Telephone: 0151 288 8090
Web: www.avantgardesalon.co.uk

Absolution Gym
Britannia Pavillion, Albert Dock, Liverpool L3 4AD
Telephone: 0151 707 9333

Spindles
Britannia Adelphi Hotel, Ranelagh Place
Liverpool L3 5UL
Telephone: 0151 709 7200
Web: www.britanniaadelphihotel.com

Skiing & Snowboarding
Runcorn Ski and Snowboard Centre
Town Park, Palace Fields, Runcorn WA7 2PS
Telephone: 01928 701965
Web: www.runcornskicentre.co.uk

Tenpin Bowling
Megabowl
Switch Island Leisure Park
Dunnings Bridge Road, Bootle L30 6TQ
Telephone: 0151 525 5676
Web: www.megabowl.co.uk

The Dogs
See Belle Vue Greyhound Stadium under The Dogs
for Manchester.

Watersports
Wirral Sailing & Watersports Centre
West Kirby Marine Lake
South Parade, West Kirby CH48 0GQ
Telephone: 0151 625 2510
Web: www.wirral.gov.uk

Surf-Tech
Crosby Marina, Liverpool L22 5PT
Telephone: 0151 920 8855
Web: www.surf-tech.co.uk
Activities: dinghy sailing, kitesurfing, waterskiing,
windsurfing

LONDON

London Visitor Centre
Arrivals Hall, Waterloo International Terminal
London SE1 7LT
Telephone: 0905 123 5000 (calls charged at £1
per minute)
Web: www.londontouristboard.com

Casinos
Gala Casinos
1 Baker Street, London W1M 1AA
Telephone: 020 7935 5013
Web: www.galacasinos.co.uk

The Grosvenor Victoria
150–162 Edgware Road, London W2 2DT
Telephone: 020 7262 7777
Web: www.rank.com

Comedy Clubs
The Comedy Store
1A Oxendon Street, London SW1Y 4EE
Telephone: 020 7344 0234
Web: www.thecomedystore.co.uk

Jongleurs
49 Lavender Gardens, Battersea
London SW11 1DJ
Telephone: 0870 240 2398
Web: www.jongleurs.co.uk

Jongleurs
Bow Wharf, 221 Grove Road
Bow, London E3 1AA
Telephone: 0870 240 2447
Web: www.jongleurs.co.uk

Jongleurs
11 East Yard, Camden Lock, London NW1 8AF
Telephone: 0870 240 2476
Web: www.jongleurs.co.uk

Flying
The Cabair Group Ltd (for a variety of locations)
Elstree Aerodrome, Borehamwood
Herts WD6 3AW
Telephone: 020 8236 2400
Web: www.cabair.com

Golf
Trent Park Public Golf Club
Bramley Road, Southgate, London N14 4UW
Telephone: 020 8367 4653
Web: www.trentparkgolfclub.com

Lee Valley Leisure Golf Course
Picketts Lock Lane, Edmonton, London N9 0AS
Telephone: 020 8803 3611

Central London Golf Centre
Burntwood Lane, Wandsworth, London SW17 0AT
Telephone: 020 8871 2468
Web: www.clgc.co.uk

Horse Racing
Ascot Racecourse
Ascot, Berkshire SL5 7JX
Telephone: 01344 876876
Web: www.ascot.co.uk

Epsom Downs Racecourse
Epsom Downs, Epsom KT18 5LQ
Telephone: 01372 470047
Web: www.epsomderby.co.uk

Windsor Racecourse
The Racecourse, Maidenhead Road
Windsor SL4 5JJ
Telephone: 0870 200 0024
Web: www.windsor-racecourse.co.uk

Kempton Park Racecourse
Kempton Park, Staines Road East
Sunbury-On-Thames TW16 5AQ
Telephone: 01372 470047
Web: www.kempton.co.uk

Sandown Park Racecourse
Portsmouth Road, Esher KT10 9AJ
Telephone: 01372 470047
Web: www.sandown.co.uk

Horse Riding
Ridgway Stables
93 Ridgway, Wimbledon Village SW19 4SU
Telephone: 020 8946 7400
Web: www.ridgwaystables.co.uk

Ross Nye Stables
8 Bathurst Mews, London W2 2SB
Telephone: 020 7262 3791
Web: www.ridingstables.co.uk

Lee Valley Riding Centre
Lee Valley Regional Park, Lee Bridge Road
Leyton E10 7QL
Telephone: 020 8556 2629
Web: www.leevalleypark.com

Hot Air Ballooning

Balloons Over London
Greenacre Lodge, Breadstone, Berkeley GL13 9HF
Telephone: 01453 810018
Web: www.balloonsoverlondon.co.uk

British School of Ballooning
Little London, Ebernoe, Nr Petworth GU28 9LF
Telephone: 01428 707307
Web: www.hotair.co.uk

Karting

Streatham Kart Raceway
390 Streatham High Road, London SW16 6HX
Telephone: 020 8677 8677
Web: www.playscape.co.uk/karting

Daytona London
Union Gate, Atlas Road, Park Royal
London NW10 6DN
Telephone: 0845 644 5501
Web: www.daytona.co.uk

Nightclubs

Carwash
Various venues in Central London, call for more information.
Telephone: 020 7403 8585
Web: www.carwash.co.uk

Strawberry Moons
15 Heddon Street, London W1B 4BF
Telephone: 020 7437 7300
Web: www.strawberrymoons.co.uk

Break for the Border
8–9 Argyll Street, London W1F 7TF
Telephone: 020 7734 5776
Web: www.bftb.com

The Clapham Grand
21–25 St John's Hill, London SW11 1TT
Telephone: 020 7223 6523
Web: www.leopardclubs.com

Walkabout
136 Shaftesbury Avenue, London W1D 5EZ
Telephone: 020 7434 0572
Web: www.walkabout.eu.com

School Disco
Telephone: 08717 177475
Web: www.schooldisco.com

Outdoor Activity Centres

Combat Games
Henfold Lakes, Beare Green, Dorking RH5 4RW
Telephone: 0870 745 0756
Web: www.ukpaintballgames.com
Activities: archery, axe throwing(!?), cross bows, mud karting, paintballing, quad biking, raft building, sling shot

Lee Leisure
84A Luton Road, Charlton, Luton LU4 9UD
Telephone: 01525 876774
Web: www.lee-leisure.co.uk
Activities: archery, clay pigeon shooting, golf

West London Shooting School
Sharvel Lane, West End Road, Northolt UB5 6RA
Telephone: 020 8845 1377
Web: www.shootingschool.co.uk
Activities: 4 x 4 off-road driving, archery, clay pigeon shooting, quad biking, Honda pilots and reverse steer, sniper rifles
No alcohol and no fancy dress.

Quad Safari
P.O. Box 101, Ware SG11 1WA
Telephone: 01920 822 977
Web: www.quadsafari.co.uk
Activities: 4 x 4 driving, quad biking

Paintball
City Paintball
Telephone: 0700 2 7529 2255
Web: www.citypaintball.com

Paintzone
393 Selsdon Road, South Croydon CR2 7AW
Telephone: 020 8688 1118
Web: www.paintzone.co.uk

Weekend Warriors (Cane End near Reading)
13–21 Crown Street, Reading RG1 2SE
Telephone: 0800 195 0637
Web: www.weekend-warriors.co.uk

National Paintball Parks
Stocking Wood, Pembridge Lane
Broxbourne EN10
and
Street End Copse
Hook Road, Rotherwick, Hook RG27
Telephone: 01707 660088
Web: www.paintballparks.co.uk

Pampering
Virgin Spa
Wandsworth Shopping Centre
Garrett Lane, London SW18 4TQ
Telephone: 020 8704 0445
Web: www.virgincosmetics.com

The Parlour
3 Ravey Street, Shoreditch, London EC2A 4QP
Telephone: 020 7729 6969
Web: www.theparlouruk.com

Apotheke 20-20
300–302 Chiswick High Road, London W4 1NP
Telephone: 020 8995 2293
Web: www.apotheke20-20.co.uk

K Spa
K West Hotel, Richmond Way, London W14 0AX
Telephone: 020 7674 1010
Web: www.k-west.co.uk

The Sanctuary
12 Floral Street, Covent Garden
London WC2E 9DH
Telephone: 0870 770 3350
Web: www.thesanctuary.co.uk

Porchester Spa
Queensway, Bayswater, London W2 5HS
Telephone: 020 7792 3980

The Phillimore Club
45 Phillimore Walk, Kensington, London W8 7RZ
Telephone: 020 7937 2882
Web: www.phillimoreclub.com

Bliss London
60 Sloane Avenue, London SW3 3DD
Telephone: 020 7584 3888
Web: www.blissworld.com

Polo
Ascot Park Polo Club
Windlesham Road, Chobham GU24 8SN
Telephone: 01276 858545
Web: www.polo.co.uk

Epsom Polo Club
Horton Country Park, Horton Lane
Epsom KT19 8PL
Telephone: 01372 749490
Web: www.epsompoloclub.co.uk

Pottery Painting

Brush 'n' Bisque-It
41 Northcote Road, London SW11 1NG
Telephone: 020 7738 9909
Web: www.brushandbisque-it.com

Brush 'n' Bisque-It
77 Church Road, Barnes SW13 9HH
Telephone: 020 8563 1515
Web: www.brushandbisque-it.com

Scuba Diving

London School of Diving
11 Power Road, London W4 5PT
Telephone: 020 8995 0002
Web: www.londonschoolofdiving.co.uk

Skiing & Snowboarding

Wycombe Summit
Abbey Barn Lane, High Wycombe HP10 9QQ
Telephone: 01494 474711
Web: www.wycombesummit.com

Snow Zone
Xscape, 602 Marlborough Gate
Milton Keynes MK9 2XS
Telephone: 01908 230260
Web: www.xscape.co.uk

Tenpin Bowling

Megabowl
142 Streatham Hill, London SW2 4RU
Telephone: 020 8678 6007
Web: www.megabowl.co.uk

Megabowl
The Rotunda, Clarence Street
Kingston Upon Thames KT1 1QP
Telephone: 020 8547 4210
Web: www.megabowl.co.uk

The Dogs

Catford Stadium
Adenmore Road, Catford, London SE6 4RJ
Telephone: 020 8690 8000
Web: www.catfordstadium.co.uk

Walthamstow Stadium
Chingford Road, London E4 8SJ
Telephone: 020 8498 3300
Web: www.wsgreyhound.co.uk

Wimbledon Stadium
Plough Lane, London SW17 0BL
Telephone: 020 8946 8000
Web: www.wimbledondogs.co.uk

Watersports

The Docklands Sailing & Watersports Centre
235A Westferry Road, Millwall Dock
Isle of Dogs, London E14 3QS
Telephone: 020 7537 2626
Web: www.dswc.org

Surrey Docks Watersports Centre
Rope Street, London SE16 7SX
Telephone: 020 7237 5555

Bella Tours
74 Alder Lodge, River Gardens
73 Stevenage Road, London SW6 6NR
Telephone: 0701 071 1855
Web: www.bella-tours.com

Classic Charters
Mimosa, Mill Stream Moorings
Mill Lane, Windsor SL4 5JH
Telephone: 01753 861494
Web: www.classic-yacht-charters.com

Winetasting
Vinopolis
1 Bank End, London SE1 9BU
Telephone: 0870 241 4040
Web: www.vinopolis.co.uk

MANCHESTER

Visitor Centre
Town Hall Extension, Lloyd Street
Manchester M60 2LA
Telephone: 0161 234 3157
Web: www.destinationmanchester.com

Casinos
Grosvenor Casino
2 Empire Street, Cheetham Hill
Manchester M3 1JA
Telephone: 0161 834 8433
Web: www.rank.com

Grosvenor Casino
35–39 George Street, Manchester M1 4HQ
Telephone: 0161 236 7121
Web: www.rank.com

Comedy Clubs
The Comedy Store
Deansgate Lock, Manchester M1 5LH
Telephone: 08705 932932
Web: www.thecomedystore.co.uk

Jongleurs
40 Chorlton Street, Manchester M1 3HW
Telephone: 0870 240 2481
Web: www.jongleurs.co.uk

Flying
Lancashire Aero Club
Barton Aerodrome, Liverpool Road
Eccles M30 7SA
Telephone: 0161 787 7326
Web: www.lancsaeroclub.co.uk

MSF Aviation
Business Aviation Centre, Hanger 7
Manchester Airport West, Manchester M90 5NE
Telephone: 0161 436 0123
Web: www.msf-aviation.com

Golf
Heaton Park Golf Centre
Middleton Road, Prestwich M25 2SW
Telephone: 0161 654 9899

Horse Racing
Haydock Park Racecourse
Newton-Le-Willows WA12 0HQ
Telephone: 01942 402624
Web: www.haydock-park.com

Chester Racecourse
Watergate Square, Chester CH1 2LY
Telephone: 01244 304600
Web: www.chester-races.co.uk

Horse Riding
Ashton Hall Equestrian Centre
Church Lane, Ashton-on-Mersey
Telephone: 0161 905 3160

Hot Air Ballooning
Balloons Over Manchester
Greenacre Lodge, Breadstone, Berkeley GL13 9HF
Telephone: 01453 810018
Web: www.balloonsovermanchester.co.uk

Karting

Karting 2000
27 Froxmer Street, Gorton M18 8EF
Telephone: 0161 231 2000
Web: www.karting2000.co.uk
Also provide clay pigeon shooting and paintball.

C K Karting
The Mill, Water Street, Radcliffe M26 3WE
Telephone: 0161 723 1010
Web: www.cat1karting.co.uk

Nightclubs

The Ritz Nightclub
Whitworth Street West, Manchester M1 5NQ
Telephone: 0161 236 4355
Web: www.theritznightclub.co.uk

Havana
42 Blackfriars Street, Manchester M3 2EQ
Telephone: 0161 832 8900

Outdoor Activity Centres

Alternative Adventure and Outdoor Activities
Service
Seddons Farm House, Newington Drive
Bury BL8 2EG
Telephone: 0161 764 3612
Web: www.altadv.co.uk
Activities: abseiling, Canadian canoeing, caving,
climbing, gorge walking, kayaking, sea-cliff
traversing

Pro Adventure
23 Castle Street, Llangollen LL20 8NY
Telephone: 01978 861912
Web: www.adventureholiday.com
Activities: abseiling, canoeing, canyoning, gorge
walking, kayaking, mountain biking, rock
climbing, white-water rafting

A6 Clay Target Centre
Reeves House Farm, Fourgates
Westhoughton, Bolton BL5 3LY
Telephone: 01942 843578
Web: www.a6ctc.co.uk
Activities: clay pigeon shooting

Paintball

Dukinfield Paintball
New Mill, Park Road, Dukinfield SK16 5LX
Telephone: 0161 214 9918

Pampering

Virgin Spa
Unit 1, The Great Northern
253 Deansgate, Manchester M3 4EN
Telephone: 0161 831 0630
Web: www.virgincosmetics.com

Le Petit Spa
Malmaison Hotel, Piccadilly, Manchester M1 3AQ
Telephone: 0161 278 1010
Web: www.malmaison.com

De Vere Mottram Hall
Wilmslow Road, Mottram St Andrew
Prestbury, Cheshire SK10 4QT
Telephone: 01625 827272
Web: www.devereonline.co.uk

LivingWell Manchester Premier
Sunlight House, Quay Street, Manchester M3 3JZ
Telephone: 0161 832 3227
Web: www.livingwell.co.uk

Scuba Diving

Subaqua1
68 Rochdale Road, Middleton
Manchester M24 2PU
Telephone: 0161 654 6768
Web: www.subaqua-1.co.uk

Skiing & Snowboarding
Runcorn Ski and Snowboard Centre
Town Park, Palace Fields, Runcorn WA7 2PS
Telephone: 01928 701965
Web: www.runcornskicentre.co.uk

Tenpin Bowling
Megabowl
White City Retail Park, Chester Road
Old Trafford, Manchester M16 0RP
Telephone: 0161 876 5084
Web: www.megabowl.co.uk

The Dogs
Belle Vue Greyhound Stadium
Kirkmanshulme Lane, Gorton M18 7BA
Telephone: 0870 840 7557
Web: www.bellevuestadium.co.uk

Watersports
Trafford Watersports Centre
Sale Water Park, Rifle Road, Sale M33 2LX
Telephone: 0161 962 0118
Web: www.thedeckersgroup.com

Salford Watersports Centre
Salford Quays, Manchester M5 2SQ
Telephone: 0161 877 7252
Web: www.salford.gov.uk/watersports

NEWCASTLE-UPON-TYNE

Tourist Information Centre
132 Grainger Street
Newcastle-upon-Tyne NE1 5AF
Telephone: 0191 277 8000
Email: tourist.info@newcastle.gov.uk
Web: www.newcastle.gov.uk
or www.tyne-online.com

Casinos
Grosvenor Casino
100 St James Boulevard
Newcastle-Upon-Tyne NE1 4BN
Telephone: 0191 260 3303
Web: www.rank.com

Comedy Clubs
The Hyena
Leazes Lane, Newcastle-Upon-Tyne NE1 4PF
Telephone: 0191 232 6030

Cornerhouse Comedy Club
The Cornerhouse Hotel
Heaton, Newcastle-Upon-Tyne NE6 5RP
Telephone: 0191 286 9038
Web: www.funnybonescomedy.co.uk

Flying
Northumbria Helicopters
Newcastle International Airport
Southside, Woolsington NE13 8BT
Telephone: 01661 871433
Web: www.northumbria-helicopters.co.uk

Northumbrian Microlights
1 Bockenfield Cottages
Felton, Morpeth NE65 9QJ
Telephone: 01670 787067
Web: www.northumbrianmicrolights.co.uk

Cleveland Flying School
Teesside Airport, Teesside BL3 1LU
Telephone: 01325 332855

Golf
Newcastle United Golf Club
60 Ponteland Road, Cowgate
Newcastle upon Tyne NE5 3JW
Telephone: 0191 286 4693

Horse Racing
Newcastle Race Course
High Gosforth Park
Newcastle-Upon-Tyne NE3 5HP
Telephone: 0191 236 2020
Web: www.newcastleracecourse.co.uk

Horse Riding
Sinderhope Pony Trekking Centre
High Sinderhope, Allenheads NE47 9SH
Telephone: 01434 685266
Web: www.sinderhopeponytrekking.co.uk

Hot Air Ballooning
Balloons Over The North
Greenacre Lodge, Breadstone, Berkeley GL13 9HF
Telephone: 01453 810018
Web: www.balloonsoverthenorth.co.uk

Karting
Karting North East Indoor
Forge Road, Dunston, Gateshead NE8 2RB
Telephone: 0191 521 4050
Web: www.kartingnortheast.com

Karting North East Outdoor
Warden Law Motorsport Centre
Sunderland SR3 2PR
Telephone: 0191 521 4050
Web: www.kartingnortheast.com

Nightclubs
Sea
Neptune House, Quayside
Newcastle-Upon-Tyne NE1 3RQ
Telephone: 0191 230 1813
Web: www.ultimateleisure.com

Blu Bambu
Grainger Court, Bigg Market
Newcastle-Upon-Tyne NE1 1UW
Telephone: 0191 261 5811
Web: www.ultimateleisure.com

Quay Club
12–20 Dean Street
Newcastle-Upon-Tyne NE1 1PG
Telephone: 0191 261 7771
Web: www.surteeshotel.co.uk

The Lounge
8–10 Neville Street
Newcastle-Upon-Tyne NE1 5EW
Telephone: 0191 261 2211

Tuxedo Princess
Hillgate Quay, Gateshead NE8 2QS
Telephone: 0191 477 8899

Outdoor Activity Centres
Turbo Venture
Pilot House, Corporation Street
Newcastle-Upon-Tyne NE4 5QF
Telephone: 0191 232 5872
Web: www.turboventure.fsnet.co.uk
Activities: abseiling, archery, assault courses, clay
pigeon shooting, flying, military off-road driving,
paintballing, paragliding, quad biking, rope
courses

Premier Leisure
The Pursuits Centre, Slaley Hall, Slaley NE47 0BY
Telephone: 01434 673100
Web: www.premleisure.com
Activities: 4 x 4 off-road Landrover driving,
archery, canoeing, clay pigeon shooting, climbing,
cross bow and air rifle shooting, mountain biking,
paintballing, quad biking, rally karting

Paintball

National Paintball Games
Opposite Teesside International Airport
Darlington DL2 1LU
Telephone: 0800 072 6969
Web: www.paintballuk.com

Top Gun Paintball
Wayside Cottage, Spawell Road
Ashwell Park, Blaydon NE21 6RS
Telephone: 0191 548 4811
Web: www.topgunpaintballuk.com

Pampering

Beauty @ Gosforth Park
Newcastle Marriott Hotel, High Gosforth Park
Newcastle-Upon-Tyne NE3 5HN
Telephone: 0191 217 1363

Swallow Hotel Newcastle Gateshead
High West Street, Gateshead NE8 1PE
Telephone: 0191 477 1105
Web: www.swallowhotels.com

The Haven Health & Beauty Salon
Copthorne Hotel, The Close, Quayside
Newcastle-Upon-Tyne NE1 3RT
Telephone: 0191 222 0333
Web: www.millenniumhotels.com

Serenity Spa @ Seaham Hall Hotel
Lord Byrons Walk, Seaham, Co. Durham SR7 7AG
Telephone: 0191 516 1550
Web: www.seaham-hall.com

Skiing & Snowboarding

Sunderland Ski Centre
Silksworth Sports Complex
Silksworth, Tyne and Wear SR3 1PD
Telephone: 0191 553 5785

Tenpin Bowling

AMF Bowling Newcastle
Westgate Road
Newcastle-Upon-Tyne
NE4 8RN
Telephone: 0191 273 0236
Web: www.amfbowling.co.uk

The Dogs

Brough Park Greyhound Stadium
The Fossway, Newcastle-Upon-Tyne NE6 2XJ
Telephone: 0191 265 8011
Web: www.thedogs.co.uk

Watersports

Teesside White Water Course & Kayaking
Tees Barrage Way, Stockton TS18 2QW
Telephone: 01642 678000
Web: www.4seasons.co.uk

Derwent Reservoir Sailing Club
Derwent Reservoir, Blanchland, Consett DH8 9PT
Telephone: 01434 675258
Web: www.derwent-rsc.co.uk

NOTTINGHAM

Tourist Information Centre
Council House, 1–4 Smithy Row
Nottingham NG1 2BY
Telephone: 0115 915 5330
Email: tourist.information@nottinghamcity.gov.uk
Web: www.nottinghamcity.gov.uk

Casinos

Gala Casinos
1–9 Bridlesmithgate, Nottingham NG1 2GR
Telephone: 0115 958 1800
Web: www.galacasinos.co.uk

Gala Casinos
4 Maid Marian Way, Nottingham NG1 6HS
Telephone: 0115 979 9288
Web: www.galacasinos.co.uk

Comedy Clubs
Jongleurs
British Waterways Warehouse, Castle Wharf
Wilford Street, Nottingham NG2 7EH
Telephone: 0870 240 2482
Web: www.jongleurs.co.uk

Flying
Phoenix Flying School
Netherthorpe Airfield, Nr Worksop S8O 3JQ
Telephone: 01909 481802
Web: www.phoenix-flying.co.uk

Golf
Bulwell Forest Golf Course
Hucknall Road, Nottingham NG6 9LQ
Telephone: 0115 976 3172

Edwalton Municipal Golf Course
Wellin Lane, Edwalton NG12 4AS
Telephone: 0115 923 4775

Horse Racing
Nottingham Racecourse
Colwick Park NG2 4BE
Telephone: 0115 958 0620
Web: www.nottinghamracecourse.co.uk

Horse Riding
College Farm Equestrian Centre
West Markham, Tuxford, Newark NG22 0PN
Telephone: 01777 870886
Web: www.haytoncollegefarm.com

Trent Valley Riding Centre
Occupation Lane, Fiskerton, Southwell NG25 0TR
Telephone: 01636 813588

Hot Air Ballooning
Balloons Over Nottingham
Greenacre Lodge, Breadstone, Berkeley GL13 9HF
Telephone: 01453 810018
Web: www.balloonsovernottingham.co.uk

Karting
Amen Corner Karting
Amen Corner, Rufford, Newark NG22 9DB
Telephone: 01623 822205
Web: www.amencornerkarting.co.uk

Express Leisure Karting
Drove Lane, Coddington, Newark NG24 2RB
Telephone: 01636 673322
Web: www.elk-racing.co.uk

Nightclubs
The Works
The Corner House, Burton Street
Nottingham NG1 4DB
Telephone: 0115 938 8780
Web: www.theworks-nottingham.co.uk

Media
The Elite Building, Queen Street
Nottingham NG1 2BL
Telephone: 0115 910 1101
Web: www.themedianightclub.co.uk

Ocean
Greyfriar Gate, Nottingham NG1 7EF
Telephone: 0115 958 0555
Web: www.oceannightclub.co.uk

The Palais
Lower Parliament Street, Nottingham NG1 3BB
Telephone: 0115 950 1075
Web: www.ukcn.com

Faces
12 Broadway, Lace Market, Nottingham NG1 1PS
Telephone: 0115 958 9000
Web: www.ukcn.com

Libertys
69–71 Upper Parliament Street
Nottingham NG1 6LD
Telephone: 0115 988 1491
Web: www.ukcn.com

Isis
Redfield Way, Nottingham NG7 2UW
Telephone: 0115 986 3211

Outdoor Activity Centres
Off Limits Corporate Events
Units 2, 3 and 9, 100 Baker Road
Newthorpe NG16 2DP
Telephone: 08700 117788
Web: www.henweekends.net
Activities: 4 x 4 driving, abseiling, archery, argo
cats, artic lorry driving, balloon flights, blindfold
tent pitching, bridge over the river why, bungee
running, clay pigeon shooting, cross bow, f1
simulator, falcolnry, fork lift trucks, gladiator
games, golf simulator, helicopter flights, Honda
pilots, horse trekking, hovercraft, human sheep
herding, human table football, It's a Knockout, JCB
driving, microquads, minefield, paintballing, quad
biking, reverse steer driving, tank driving, target
archery

Buggyland II
The National Watersports Centre
Holme Pierrepont, Adbolton Lane
Nottingham NG12 2LU
Telephone: 0115 921 2584
Web: www.buggyland2.com
Activities: archery, laser clay pigeon shooting, mud
buggies, quad biking

Adrenalin Jungle
Sherwood Forest, Nottingham
Telephone: 01623 883831
Web: www.paintball-jungle.co.uk
Activities: 4 x 4 driving, clay pigeon shooting,
military vehicle driving, off-road karting,
paintballing, pony trekking, quad biking

Paintball
Skirmish Paintball Games
Moorfield Farm, Ollerton Road
Oxton, Southwell NG25 0RE
Telephone: 0115 965 7830
Web: www.skirmish.org

Commando Paintball
Nottingham
Telephone: 0115 984 5500
Web: www.nottinghampaintball.co.uk

Pampering
Virgin Spa
The Cornerhouse, Burton Street
Nottingham NG1 4DB
Telephone: 0115 934 2230
Web: www.virgincosmetics.com

Eden Hall Day Spa
Elston Village, Newark, NG23 5PG
Telephone: 01636 525555
Web: www.edenhallspa.co.uk

Hall of Beauty
Holmes Place, Low Level Station
London Road, Nottingham NG2 3AE
Telephone: 0115 947 2906
Web: www.holmesplace.co.uk

Skiing & Snowboarding
The Snowdome
Leisure Island, River Drive, Tamworth B79 7ND
Telephone: 0870 500 0011
Web: www.snowdome.co.uk

Tenpin Bowling
AMF Bowling Nottingham
Barker Gate, Nottingham NG1 1JZ
Telephone: 0115 950 5588
Web: www.amfbowling.co.uk

The Dogs
Nottingham Greyhound Stadium
Colwick Park NG2 4BE
Telephone: 0115 910 3333
Web: www.nottinghamdogs.com

Watersports
National Watersports Centre
Adbolton Lane, Holme Pierrepont
Nottingham NG12 2LU
Telephone: 0115 982 1212
Web: www.nationalsports.co.uk

SHEFFIELD

Tourist Information Centre
1 Tudor Square, Surrey Street, Sheffield S1 2LA
Telephone: 0114 221 1900
Web: www.sheffieldcity.co.uk

Casinos
Grosvenor Casino
Queens Road, Sheffield S2 4DF
Telephone: 0114 275 7433
Web: www.rank.com

Flying
Sheffield Aero Club
Netherthorpe Airfield, Thorpe Salvin
Worksop S80 3JQ
Telephone: 01909 475233
Web: www.sheffair.f9.co.uk

Golf
Beauchief Golf Course
Abbey Lane, Sheffield S8 0DB
Telephone: 0114 236 7274
Web: www.beauchiefgolfcourse.co.uk

Horse Racing
Doncaster Racecourse
Leger Way, Doncaster DN2 6BB
Telephone: 01302 304207
Web: www.doncaster-racecourse.com

Horse Riding
Low Ash Riding Centre
Stubbing Lane, Worrall S35 0AP
Telephone: 0114 234 3577

Hot Air Ballooning
See Balloons Over Nottingham under Hot Air
Ballooning for Nottingham who also fly over
Sheffield.

Karting
Parkwood Karting
Parkwood Road, Sheffield S3 8AH
Telephone: 0114 279 9666
Web: www.parkwoodkarting.com

Nightclubs
Republic
112 Arundel Street, Sheffield S1 1DJ
Telephone: 0114 276 6777
Web: www.gatecrasher.co.uk

Bed
33 London Road, Sheffield
Telephone: 0114 276 6777
Web: www.gatecrasher.co.uk

Kingdom
1 Burgess Street, Barkers Pool, Sheffield S1 2HF
Telephone: 0114 278 8811
Web: www.kingdom-nightclub.com

Club Wow
Valley Centertainment Park
Broughton Lane, Sheffield S9 2EP
Telephone: 0114 243 5670
Web: www.firstleisure.com

Outdoor Activity Centres
Parson House Outdoor Pursuits Centre
Longshaw, Nr Fox House, Sheffield S11 7TZ
Telephone: 01433 631017
Web: www.parsonhouse.co.uk
Activities: abseiling, canoeing, caving, climbing,
kayaking, orienteering

Demon Wheelers
Unit 1 Clarence Works, 30–36 Burton Road
Sheffield S3 8BX
Telephone: 0114 270 0330
Web: www.demonwheelers.co.uk
Activities: 4 x 4 off-road driving, abseiling, archery,
blindfold driving, bungee run, bouncy boxing,
bouncy castle, canoeing, caving, chuckle buggies,
clay pigeon shooting, climbing, cross bow,
gladiator duel, hovercraft, inflatable obstacle
course, It's a Knockout, laser clay shooting, laser
pistols and rifles, minefield game, mountain
biking, off-road racing buggies, paintballing, quad
biking, reverse steer car, rodeo bull, shooting
gallery, waterfall abseiling

Paintball
Ambush Paintball Games Ltd
244 Providence Road, Walkley Bank
Sheffield S6 5BH
Telephone: 0114 285 2850
Web: www.ambushpaintballgames.co.uk

Skirmish Paintball Games
Aizlewoods Mill, Nursery Street, Sheffield S3 8GG
Telephone: 0114 249 3119
Web: www.skirmish.org

Pampering
The Sensory
LivingWell Sheffield Premier
Victoria Quays, Furnival Road, Sheffield S4 7YA
Telephone: 0114 252 5566
Web: www.livingwell.co.uk

Marriott Leisure, Health & Beauty Club
Kenwood Road, Nether Edge, Sheffield S7 1NQ
Telephone: 0114 250 5616
Web: www.marriotthotels.co.uk

Skiing & Snowboarding
Sheffield Ski Village
Vale Road, Parkwood Springs, Sheffield S3 9SJ
Telephone: 0114 276 9459
Web: www.sheffieldskivillage.co.uk

Tenpin Bowling
AMF Bowling Sheffield
Sicey Avenue, Firth Park, Sheffield S5 6NF
Telephone: 0114 242 5152
Web: www.amfbowling.co.uk

The Dogs
Sheffield Sport Stadium
Peniston Road, Sheffield S6 2DE
Telephone: 0114 234 3074
Web: www.owlertonstadium.co.uk

Watersports

Sheffield Cable Waterski Centre
Rother Valley Country Park
Mansfield Road, Wales Bar S31 8PE
Telephone: 0114 251 1717
Web: www.sheffieldcablewaterski.com

Rother Valley Watersports
Rother Valley Country Park
Mansfield Road, Wales Bar S26 5PQ
Telephone: 0114 247 1453
Web: www.rothervalley.f9.co.uk

MORE ALTERNATIVE ACTIVITIES

Amusement Parks

Alton Towers
Alton, Staffordshire ST10 4DB
Telephone: 0870 520 4060
Web: www.altontowers.com

American Adventure
Ilkeston, Derbyshire DE7 5SX
Telephone: 0845 330 2929
Web: www.americanadventure.com

Blackpool Pleasure Beach
Ocean Boulevard, South Promenade
Blackpool FY4 1PL
Telephone: 01253 403223
Web: www.blackpoolpleasurebeach.com

Chessington World of Adventures
Leatherhead Road, Chessington KT9 2NE
Telephone: 0870 444 7777
Web: www.chessington.com

Disneyland Paris
Web: www.disneylandparis.com

Drayton Manor Park
Drayton Manor, Tamworth B78 3TW
Telephone: 01827 287979
Web: www.draytonmanor.co.uk

Thorpe Park
Staines Road, Chertsey, Surrey KT16 8PN
Telephone: 0870 444 4466
Web: www.thorpepark.com

Bungee Jumping

UK Bungee Club (various locations)
122 Leeds Road, Lost House, Wakefield WF3 3LP
Telephone: 07000 286433
Web: www.ukbungee.com

Caving

National Caving Organisation
Web: www.nca.org.uk

Cheddar Caves and Gorge
Cheddar, Somerset BS27 3QF
Telephone: 01934 742343
Web: www.cheddarcaves.co.uk

Driving Experiences

Aintree Racing Drivers School
Three Sisters Race Circuit
Bryn Road, Wigan WN4 8DD
Telephone: 01942 270230
Web: www.racing-school.co.uk

Castle Combe Racing School
Castle Combe Circuit, Chippenham SN14 7EY
Telephone: 01249 782417
Web: www.castlecomberacingschool.co.uk

Thruxton Motorsports Centre
Thruxton Circuit, Andover SP11 8PW
Telephone: 01264 882222
Web: www.thruxtonracing.co.uk

Wild Tracks Offroad Activity Park
Chippenham Road, Kennett, Newmarket CB8 7QJ
Telephone: 01638 751918
Web: www.wildtracksltd.co.uk

Knockhill Racing Circuit
Just by Dunfermline, Fife, Scotland KY12 9TF
Telephone: 01383 723337
Web: www.knockhill.com

Mithral Racing
Goodwood Motor Circuit, Chichester PO18 0PH
Telephone: 01243 528815
Web: www.mithral.co.uk

Silverstone Rally School
Silverstone Park, Silverstone, Northants NN12 8TJ
Telephone: 01327 857413
Web: www.silverstonerally.co.uk

Hang Gliding
The British Hang Gliding and Paragliding
Association Ltd, The Old Schoolroom
Loughborough Road, Leicester LE4 5PJ
Telephone: 0870 870 6490
Web: www.bhpa.co.uk

It's A Knockout
Banzai Events
Stratton Court Barn, Pool Farm
Stratton Audley, Bicester OX27 9RJ
Telephone: 01869 278199
Web: www.banzaievents.com
Activities: archery, argo cat, blind driving, clay
shooting, croquet, falconry, helicopters, Honda
pilot racing buggies, hovercraft, It's a Knockout,
karts, kites, power turn rally driving, quad biking,
reverse steer, rodeo bull, sheepdogs, shooting

Outdoor Concerts & Theatre
Burghley House
Stamford PE9 3JY
Telephone: 01780 752451
Web: www.burghley.co.uk

Blenheim Palace
Woodstock, Oxfordshire OX20 1PX
Telephone: 01993 811325
Web: www.blenheimpalace.com

Leeds Castle
Maidstone, Kent ME17 1PL
Telephone: 01622 765400
Web: www.leeds-castle.com

Ragley Hall
Alcester, Warwickshire B49 5NJ
Telephone: 01789 762090
Web: www.ragleyhall.com

Kenwood House
The Iveagh Bequest, Kenwood
Hampstead Lane, London NW3 7JR
Telephone: 020 8348 1286
Web: www.english-heritage.org.uk

The Open Air Theatre
The Iron Works, Inner Circle
Regent's Park, London NW1 4NR
Telephone: 020 7486 2431
Web: www.open-air-theatre.org.uk

Minack Theatre and Visitor Centre
Porthcurno, Penzance, Cornwall TR19 6JU
Telephone: 01736 810181
Web: www.minack.com

Party Boats
Parties Afloat
Gas Street Basin, Gas Street, Birmingham B1 2JT
Telephone: 0121 236 7057

Ropes Courses
Adventure Rope Co.
Fern Hollow, Ruyton, Shrewsbury SY4 1JT
Telephone: 01939 261122
Web: www.adventurerope.co.uk

High Ropes Adventure
Linwood Warren, Legsby Road, Market Rasen
Lincolnshire LN8 3DZ
Telephone: 01526 354182
Web: www.highropesadventure.com

Sailing
Formula 1 Sailing
Haslar Marina, Haslar Road, Gosport PO12 1NU
Telephone: 02392 522388
Web: www.formula1sailing.com

Ahoy! Scotland
63 High Street, East Linton
East Lothian EH40 3BQ
Telephone: 07808 634956
Web: www.ahoy-scotland.co.uk

Yacht Charter
Greencroft, Manchester Road, Sway SO49 6AS
Telephone: 01590 681390
Web: www.yachtcharteruk.com

Surfing
National Surfing Centre
Newquay, Cornwall
Telephone: 01736 360250
Web: www.nationalsurfingcentre.com

Gower Surfing
6 Slade Road, Newton, Swansea SA3 4UE
Telephone: 01792 360370
Web: www.gowersurfing.com

Welsh Surfing Federation Surf School
Llangennith, Swansea SA3 1HU
Telephone: 01792 386426
Web: www.wsfsurfschool.co.uk

Survival Weekends
Survival School
Northwood, Poltimore, Exeter EX4 0AR
Telephone: 01392 460312
Web: www.survivalschool.co.uk

UK Survival School
Seymour House, 24 East Street, Hereford HR1 2LU
Telephone: 01432 376751
Web: www.uksurvivalschool.co.uk

White-Water Rafting
The English White-Water Rafting Committee
c/o Current Trends, Adbolton Lane
Nottingham NG2 5AS
Telephone: 0115 981 8844
Web: www.currenttrends.co.uk

Index